INFLUENCE IN ACTION™
for CEOs

Written by

Robert J. Smith, MFA

and CEOs:

Amber R. Carlson, Paul J. Simino, Joseph Iturria, Loreta Tarozaite,
Jennifer Sheets, Tali Arviv, M.D., Wayne Tupuola, Carol Ann Langford,
Douglas S. King, Cristopher Craig, Alex Hernandez

Influence in Action™ for CEOs
1st Edition. 2025

Hardback ISBN: 978-1-965538-11-1
Paperback ISBN: 978-1-965538-12-8
E-book ISBN: 978-1-965538-13-5
Audiobook ISBN: 978-1-965538-14-2

Book Layout © 2025, **Published by:** RJS Pro Publishing and Amazon Publishing Center.

"You can't build a reputation on what you are going to do."

— **Henry Ford**

Dedication

INFLUENCE IN ACTION™ *for CEOs* is dedicated to the late, great Lee Iacocca who taught us that second best is not near good enough. Mr. Iacocca also taught us that second in command is not in command, and instead, it is only a breath away from the street.

This book is also dedicated to every CEO, everyone who wants to someday become a CEO, and everyone who lives with, tolerates and provides support to a CEO.

Acknowledgments

I would like to thank Sharon Roznowski, M.Ed. for her patience and support, during the creation of this book.

I would like to thank Amber R. Carlson for being such a go-getter as well as Paul J. Simino, Joseph Iturria, Loreta Tarozaite, Jennifer Sheets, Tali Arviv M.D., Wayne Tupuola, Carol Ann Langford, Douglas S. King, Christopher Craig, Alex Hernandez, and Ron Wallace for their thoughtful contributions to ***INFLUENCE IN ACTION*^{TM} *for CEOs***.

I would also like to thank all of my teams who have diligently worked on this important book project from start to finish.

Contents

Foreword

As President of UPS International, where I led operations across more than 200 countries and managed a team of 60,000 employees, I was one of seven executives on the management committee that oversaw the day-to-day operations of UPS, a ninety-billion-dollar company with 435,000 employees.

In retirement, I wrote my first book called ***LEADERSHIP LESSONS FROM A UPS DRIVER, DELIVERING A CULTURE OF WE, NOT ME©***. Too often leadership lessons are overthought and become complicated. My book is grounded on real life lessons in the leadership role with one quote in my book that simply states, "*To build a high-performance team, use simple principles within a basic structure that everyone can easily understand.*"

It was published and marketed through one of the largest companies in the world. There were a lot of hard lessons learned, and a lot of money spent on promotion, with little return on investment. I wish I would have known Robert Smith way back then.

As an author of five books and with one more near completion, I had difficulty selling books. That is until I met Robert Smith. His marketing experience, along with his rock-solid strategies and continuing advice has helped me tremendously.

Smitty has worked with me on a book I wrote called ***AMERICAN MADNESS, THE ASSAULT ON AMERICAN VALUES©***. I was so upset about what was going on in our great country that I wrote a book about the Marxist regime that is openly attacking America with woke's weapons of mass destruction. Critical Race Theory, (CRT), Cancel Culture, Gender Identity, Social Emotional Learning, biological males invading female sports and in bathrooms, locker rooms, and so much more.

The story needed to be told and I needed help. A friend loved the book and introduced me to Smitty. Once I applied Smitty's methods to my work, *__AMERICAN MADNESS__*" became known worldwide and recognized on Amazon as a **#1 International Best Seller**.

Of course, there is much more to life than sales volume, and even rising to the top of a major corporation. We all have a duty to preserve our American values and to contribute to our communities. It's refreshing to see how the CEOs in this book contribute to society, just as Smitty does with his Junior Patriots™ nonprofit organization.

As for me, I've been able to make significant contributions as a police officer, developer, restaurateur, and public servant. I was fortunate enough to be appointed by the Governor of Georgia to chair the Commission for the Creation of the City of Milton, Georgia. I was able to act as the inaugural leader to establish city infrastructure and services.

Just as Smitty founded the Junior Patriots™ nonprofit and serves as that charity's President, I am proud to have served on several nonprofit boards. I believe that philanthropy is a must for every successful CEO.

Prologue

Thank you for investing your time in this installment of our #1 Best Selling **INFLUENCE IN ACTION™** series. This book is designed for CEOs and leaders who are weary of unproven ideas that go unimplemented. Our purpose is straightforward: to equip you with practical, proven influence strategies that you can apply immediately—helping you build momentum with early wins, scale what works, and create a business legacy that endures. Every strategy outlined in this series has been validated through the bold and consistent **ACTION** taken by each CEO who has shared their insights with you.

"The secret of getting ahead is getting started."
— **Mark Twain**

We'll provide you with tested strategies that you can implement right away to achieve measurable wins. From there, you can build momentum to exceed your short-term, medium-term, and long-term objectives. It's up to you to take the initiative, harness early victories, and maintain that momentum for the life of your business. When we all excel in this, we create a legacy that outlasts us.

Leave any excuses to your competition. You don't need them.

Think you're too young? The creator of your *INFLUENCE IN ACTION™* series completed more oil changes in a single month than anyone else in the Motor City at that time, 4,464 at the age of 18 for Mobil Oil, a record that remains unmatched.

He then earned the #1 Home Market Merchandising route for Coca-Cola in Sarasota, Florida, at just 20 years old.

Is the weather in your area less than ideal? Those Mobil Oil changes were performed in the depths of winter in Detroit, Michigan. Two years later, the run to #1 at Coca-Cola involved emptying a truck on a beach route after other drivers were called back, just before the coast was evacuated for Hurricane Elena. Yes, a real Category 3 hurricane with 125 MPH winds, long before Lieutenant Dan and Forrest Gump made working in such conditions famous.

Dealing with an injury or a career change? After sustaining an injury at Coke following a monumental challenge, your series creator transitioned to a white-collar financial services career and rapidly set every sales and production record for a branch manager at BankAtlantic, which later merged into BB&T and subsequently TRUIST.

Struggling to manage a team? Every one of those BankAtlantic records was surpassed in short order with a team of inexperienced salespeople from diverse backgrounds.

Have a family to provide for? Your series creator set a 64-year record at John Hancock by earning his professional designations through the American College in just 13 months, compared to the typical 48-84 months. Thirty-four years later, that record still stands. If it holds for two more years, we'll reach 100 years, remarkable for a skinny kid from Livonia, Michigan.

Great at solo work but struggle in a team? Your series creator had the privilege of working with an exceptional team at a reputable company, consistently qualifying for the Million Dollar Round Table (MDRT®) during New York Life's *50th consecutive year of MDRT® leadership.* Each of us who qualified was honored to have our names engraved on a plaque in the lobby of the New York Life building on Madison Avenue.

Facing personal hardships? Divorce, custody battles, medical issues, or life-changing injuries? Your series creator has experienced all of that while simultaneously leading Mutual of New York (MONY), The Equitable Assurance Society, and AXA Financial in global production. This was while managing the equivalent of driving around the world twice to care for children in two different states and attending every school and sporting event they were involved in.

Think you're too old? Your series creator was 53 when he earned his first **#1 Best Seller** as part of ***SALES GENIUS #1***, which surpassed The Wolf of Wall Street's sales book, ***THE WAY OF THE WOLF***, released at the same time.

Way too old? Your INFLUENCE IN ACTIONTM series creator was 60 when he wrote the #1 Best Seller, INFLUENCE IN ACTIONTM GAINS PROVEN RESULTS AND DRIVES SALES, and the #1 Best Seller, INFLUENCE IN ACTIONTM BRINGS MORE BUSINESS TO ENTREPRENEURS. Now at 61 with this book's release, he has also been medically declared "Totally and Permanently Disabled."

Run out of excuses yet? If so, reach out to me through the QR code in the About the Author section at the end of this chapter. You'll achieve the results you deserve. If you still have excuses, contact me directly. Together, we'll find a way to overcome any barrier in your path. You, your family, and your stakeholders deserve results, not excuses.

If you've exhausted your excuses, read this book. Learn from our co-authors who are CEOs, record-breakers, and industry leaders. Connect with their stories and strategies, and put them into action. Don't hesitate, get to work.

Do so, and you'll find yourself on top. You'll either be ranked #1 in your field or among the top 1% in your industry. You'll be amazed at the gains you make, and how quickly you realize them.

Jump in and get started. If you prefer using the Table of Contents to locate the person or topic that resonates with you, go ahead. Just ensure you take immediate ACTION with the strategies outlined in each chapter.

If you choose to read this book sequentially, from start to finish, you can't go wrong with Amber R. Carlson. I've known Amber for nearly a year and have witnessed the tremendous results she consistently delivers for her clients and her business.

You'll find the same is true for every co-author in *INFLUENCE IN ACTIONTM for CEOs*. Like Amber, I've gotten to know Paul J. Simino, Joseph Iturria, Loreta Tarozaite, Jennifer Sheets, Tali Arviv M.D., Wayne Tupuola, Carol Ann Langford, Douglas S. King, Christopher Craig, Alex Hernandez, and Ron Wallace. These Presidents and CEOs bring years of experience running successful companies, both public and private. They are generously sharing their success strategies with you, hoping you can match or surpass the achievements we all enjoy.

All we ask in return is that you put the proven influence and success strategies outlined in this book into *ACTION*. When you do, you will see optimal results.

If you need assistance, feel free to reach out to any of us through the contact information provided at the end of each chapter. Whatever strategies you gain, do yourself a favor and put your *INFLUENCE IN ACTIONTM*.

"Everyone has ideas—you, I, the gang in the mailroom—even our competitors, bless 'em. What really counts is what you do with them."

— Stan Lee

CHAPTER ONE

The Hidden KPI:
How CEOs Turn Influence into Legacy

By Amber Carlson

Let me share a story with two possible outcomes.

Picture this: you are standing on a stage with a glass of champagne in hand. Your C-suite team, board of directors, VPs, and other key figures in your organization raise a toast to you and your achievements. Detailed accounts of the revenue growth, market expansion, and accolades you have amassed over your career are celebrated by the group. They lift their glasses to wish you well as you transition to the next chapter of your life in retirement. But here's the question lingering in their minds: "Now what?" What will happen to the organization, their departments, and their roles now that you are no longer at the helm?

One possible outcome is that the company begins to scramble. With no ready successor, burned-out managers, and overall confusion, it starts to crumble and slide into complacency. Alternatively, the leaders may confidently step forward, equipped with the skills, tools, resources, and lessons that prepare them to tackle new challenges.

I'm sure you would choose the second outcome, who wouldn't? I have spoken with numerous CEOs at the end of their careers, and they all agree that their people are the most important aspect of their businesses. However, in the daily grind of leadership, we often become obsessed with measuring growth, margin, and valuation. Yet, the KPI we seldom track is leadership legacy, the measurable strength of the leaders you leave behind. The hidden KPI is how consistently you use your influence to build trust, ownership, and capability in others, ensuring the business continues to thrive even when you're no longer in the room.

We aren't just discussing succession planning or bench strength, like who can take over board relations or capitalize on acquisitions. We are focused on developing leaders throughout the organization who can lead, motivate, and influence others. This is what we mean by a leadership legacy. One of my favorite quotes on this subject, often attributed to either John Quincy Adams or Dolly Parton, though no one is quite sure, rings true: **"If your actions create a legacy that inspires others to dream more, learn more, do more, and become more, you are an excellent leader."**

Leadership legacy is more than a title or charisma; it encompasses the behaviors necessary to inspire others to act in unison toward a shared goal. Motivating others to take action is the essence of leadership. However, leaders don't need to oversee every action, movement, and decision. That's not leadership; that's micromanagement, which ultimately undermines personal accountability, ownership, and empowerment. We need leaders who create other leaders. (Yes, I said it twice.) Consider this: what would happen if you vanished from the org chart tomorrow? Would your team continue moving in the right direction because of the leaders you have developed, or would everything stall and fall apart?

Call it motivation or inspiration, but ultimately, the resource leaders leverage to encourage action is their influence. Influence is the ability to shape what others think, feel, decide, and ultimately do over time. Through a leader's influence, team behavior, choices, and beliefs can change. It can be positive or negative, loud or quiet, inspirational or fear-based. Just as Martin Luther King Jr.'s commitment to nonviolence inspired millions to rethink segregation, fear-based leadership can lead teams to hide problems, protect egos, and make costly decisions. Thus, we must wield influence carefully for the benefit of our people and the future.

Influence is how we move mountains, and it all starts with one simple truth: leaders must build trust. Stephen M.R. Covey argues in The Speed of Trust that trust predicts speed, and I've witnessed this firsthand. I recall an organization I worked with that was so siloed and distrustful that they hired an outside firm to develop a program at a cost of over 2 million dollars, only to discover that another department had been working on the exact same initiative for the past eight months, and theirs was better. What a waste!

You might think this could never happen to you, but I challenge you to consider: What don't you know? What might others be withholding from you? How well do you truly understand the goals of department leaders? I've overheard the COO say behind closed doors that they "don't reveal too much" to the CEO to avoid micromanagement. That's a scary thought, especially when the CEO has to present to the board of directors. That same organization filed for Chapter 11 two years later. Forgive my sarcasm, but it's no wonder. We don't have to remain trapped in ignorance about what's happening in our organization; instead, we can harness trust to influence others to be honest with us, open with us, and communicate directly. We will listen without bulldozing or sugar-coating.

Next, we must instill the virtue of personal ownership throughout the organization. The powerful book *Extreme Ownership* by Jocko Willink and Leif Babin emphasizes that ownership ultimately rests with you, the CEO. Whether it's ensuring payroll is processed on time, fulfilling customer orders accurately, or emptying the office wastebaskets, the responsibility lies with you. Instilling personal ownership in our team begins with our own example. When the team sees us take responsibility for our mistakes, they are more likely to do the same. I once met a CEO who exemplified this by sending a company-wide email detailing three things he did right and three things he did wrong in his end-of-year summary. He was amazed by the number of responses from managers and directors across the company who shared their own successes and failures. He inspired transparency through his influence.

However, there's an uncomfortable truth about this hidden KPI of leadership legacy: you are its limit. As senior leaders, we set the ceiling for capacity. Our egos, need for control, and reluctance to delegate create barriers to opportunity. But this isn't all doom and gloom; it means we have the power to change it. Remember, if every significant decision depends solely on you, then you're not cultivating leaders, you're fostering doers. There's a fascinating business model that challenges traditional hierarchical structures called Holacracy. In Holacracy, Brian Robertson describes a system where authority is distributed through clear roles and agreed-upon rules, preventing decisions from bottlenecking at the top. You don't need to adopt it entirely to grasp the lesson. Your role is to develop leaders who can decide, act, learn, and report independently.

Two ways to raise the ceiling are through the relationships you cultivate and your communication style. Relationships must be intentional, but not every connection needs to be deep. As the CEO, you can show respect and kindness to everyone in your company and beyond. Being fully present, remembering what you learn, and recalling it during future encounters demonstrates that you genuinely care. Herb Kelleher, co-founder and long-time CEO of Southwest Airlines, was known for his remarkable ability to remember details; former employees shared that he would greet them by name even a year after their first meeting. However, you don't need to memorize every detail to make an impact. The intentional relationships you cultivate should be viewed as investments. Remember, those who gain proximity also gain possibilities. You are the one who provides opportunities for others. Access to you signals that the person matters and that you recognize their potential for leadership. Do you see the future of your organization reflected in the relationships you have now? Could you miss an opportunity by keeping your circle too tight? Then it's time to broaden your network, or as another CEO friend of mine puts it, "start a stretch program for yourself." Look for emerging leaders and invite them to strategic meetings or, even better, grab coffee to learn who they really are. Focus on deepening your immediate relationships while also expanding your new connections.

How well you communicate directly influences your ability to build relationships. We seek authentic connections, not transactional or conditional ones. Think mentor/mentee, sensei/student, or guru/disciple. While we aren't parting the Red Sea, we aim to nurture relationships that foster growth. We're not just adding another pair of hands; we're inspiring someone who we hope will one day walk in our shoes and forge their own path. Your words, tone, and timing can either encourage or diminish someone's willingness to lead. This requires us to be hyper-vigilant in how we communicate bad news, engage with those we disagree with, or address failures. We must transform moments into lessons by leading with curiosity first. By asking questions, understanding the why, and exploring alternative approaches, we can cultivate a leader mentality in others. As CEOs, it's easy to operate in command mode, issuing expectations. When we shift to a curiosity-first approach, we draw out the potential in others, enabling them to make decisions, see possibilities, and take ownership of outcomes.

However, let's be clear: curiosity isn't abdication. It's about creating a space for others to elevate their thinking and responsibility.

People remember the moments when a mentor or senior leader gave them the space to grow. In many leadership workshops I've led for managers and directors, I often hear stories of leaders who provided opportunities to learn, fail, and develop. These narratives frequently conclude with, "and that was the best leader I've ever had." The same is true for the CEOs I've worked with over the years. One common story is when a CEO, early in their career, was thrust into a role or project they didn't feel prepared for, yet their leader believed in them and encouraged them to take that leap. These CEOs often credit that moment as a pivotal point in their careers that led them to where they are today. That's the power we can share – your legacy.

Let's discuss how to create a legacy engine that leverages your influence to develop leaders. Looking across your organization, where should you focus your energy? Should you concentrate on your immediate direct reports in the C-suite? We find that the most overloaded and underdeveloped group, often promoted based on performance, is actually your front-line managers. Depending on your organization's size, this could range from the office manager of your practice to the department leads in your plant. These individuals bridge the gap between your direction to the executive team and the front-line workers delivering services or products to customers. Like a game of telephone, your influence doesn't flow directly *to* your employees; it cascades *through* layers of leadership. If one layer misaligns with your vision and guidance, the entire structure can collapse under uncertainty, misdirection, and confusion. Your leadership teams either replicate your best behaviors and influence or amplify your worst. Your managers aren't just another layer; they are your legacy engine, the leaders you'll leave behind to nurture and advance the company.

One effective way to invest in your legacy engine is to host a monthly front-line leader huddle. Gather 10–15 managers, share the one priority you want them to focus on, ask what obstacles they face, and conclude with one decision they can make independently. Then, follow up on their execution. That's how your influence transforms into capability, not just direction.

Now, for some, this thought can be intimidating. Growing others to lead the company means preparing my replacement. Does that make me obsolete? Yes and no. We want our future leaders to be strong enough to thrive independently; that's growth. Yet, we also wish to be honored and remembered for guiding the way, forging paths, and laying the groundwork for them to follow; that's legacy. So how do we transition our managers from an organizational layer to a legacy-engine? There are three C's that can help you, and they all depend on you (remember ownership): Coaching, Connecting, and Culture.

Coaching

Help people think, not just comply.

Coaching. It's a familiar concept. We often hear, "Be a coach, not a director." However, coaching goes beyond giving instructions and encouragement. It isn't merely about providing feedback or answers; it's about asking questions that guide others to their own conclusions. For those of us who enjoy telling others what to do (guilty!), this represents a challenging shift in mindset. Fun fact: the term "coach" originates from the four-wheeled carriage pulled by horses, which helped transport someone from one place to another. When we adopt our coaching role, we say, "Let me help you think this through," rather than, "Here's what you need to do," as highlighted in Sir John Whitmore's book, *Coaching for Performance*, which I greatly admire. As leaders, when we coach managers, we focus on empowering them to make informed decisions through inquiry. This fosters personal ownership and growth. Ultimately, coaching is what you do when you choose to become less necessary or less of the hero. It's about teaching others to think independently, reducing their reliance on you for every decision, and strategically setting up the foundation to step back and let others shine. It's about building an intentional legacy.

Connecting

Proximity that signals possibility.

Connecting is the glue. When it comes to listening and learning someone's story, I always emphasize the importance of being "wildly curious and genuinely interested," a lesson I learned from my mentor, thanks, Meg! We all have opportunities to shake hands and make small talk, but what truly matters in connection is the authentic relationships and moments we build. As a leader, how you allocate your time communicates what is important to you. Whether you focus on reviewing P&L statements, balance sheets, performance dashboards, and forecasts, or spend time listening during town halls, conducting site visits, meeting new employees, and hearing their stories, where you invest your time matters. Without genuine connection, CEOs can lose sight of their organization's heartbeat, risking disengagement and a weakened leadership legacy. Your presence is irreplaceable; it's the one thing you can't delegate and what your team values most (without overdoing it). While your assistant can schedule meetings, only you can show up to connect and make your team feel that their stories matter. It's surprising how rarely this occurs, and how unaware many CEOs are of this reality. A 2023 study by Forbes Coaches Council on the Leadership Trust Index found that CEOs rated themselves as 29% more trustworthy than their teams perceived them to be. [source: Blakey, J. (2023, February 14). *Measuring trust using the Leadership Trust Index*. Forbes

Coaches Council]. Ouch! We may have good intentions or believe we are connecting, but what do our people truly think? One of my favorite examples involves a CEO who held a different lunch meeting each day with various staff members, from C-suite leaders to line-shift managers, throughout the year. He spent that time learning their stories, dreams, and lives, and, rightly so, he always treated them to lunch. A smooth and effective way to connect.

Culture

The behaviors you tolerate and repeat.

Culture is where vision meets action. It encompasses the shared beliefs, values, behaviors, and unwritten rules that shape how individuals act within an organization. You hold the keys to how culture is shaped and maintained. You can't simply compile a list of company values and claim to have a culture. In fact, it is the moments in between, the side conversations, attitudes towards challenges, approaches to conflict, and explanations behind decisions, that define the inner workings of company culture.

What is your North Star, and how do you follow it? Your North Star is the clear, steadfast point that guides decisions and actions. It represents a non-negotiable belief or value you refuse to compromise for short-term gains. This is the filter you use when pressure mounts.

One CEO exemplifies this perfectly. Her company's top value was "Tell the truth, even when it's hard," a principle put to the test when she discovered an unnoticed mistake on a major contract. She shared with me that the easy choice would have been to remain silent and meet shareholder expectations. Instead, she followed her North Star, contacted the client to explain the error, and revised the contract. This decision became legendary within the company and secured a long-term deal with that client for over two decades. The North Star value wasn't just a phrase on their website; it was a genuine commitment that shaped their culture and became part of their legacy.

The final piece of the hidden KPI puzzle is the most crucial denominator. Without it, true leadership and legacy creation become nearly impossible. I've alluded to this throughout the chapter. If you want to create a lasting legacy and serve as a catalyst for growth, change, improvement, and development, humility is essential. We don't seek silent obedience; we want shared ownership. We don't desire fleeting headlines; we aspire for enduring reputations. This isn't about self-deprecation, false modesty, or undermining your hard work. It's about ensuring your company thrives beyond the removal of your nameplate or email signature. Arrogance asks, "How will they remember *me*?" Humility inquires, "How can I ensure they'll succeed when I'm gone?" This is the essence of legends. In Joseph Campbell's *The Hero With A Thousand Faces* (a fantastic read!), his mentor appears early in the story as a protective and guiding force who prepares the hero for what lies ahead, yet doesn't walk the entire path. This embodiment of support conveys, "You're not ready yet, but I can help you prepare, and then you'll need to continue without me." As a CEO or senior leader, you have the power to unlock others' potential and guide them toward their own greatness. In business, we carve out our success; in leadership, we cultivate the success of others. After all, "Before you can pass the torch, you must first have a torch worth passing."

If you'd like to learn more about developing an intentional leadership legacy, please visit www.igniteyourlegacyseries.com for books, information, and experiences on this topic, or contact my team and me at www.archwaylearningsolutions.com for additional workshops and resources (I love this stuff!). Over the past 15 years, I've studied legacy, learning from CEOs in their 60s and 70s, new CEOs in their 20s, and 90-

year-olds reflecting on their past, as well as young students crafting their futures. The biggest lesson I've learned is that our legacy is shaped by our actions every day, in every interaction, and with every person we meet. It is up to us how we show up, what we instill, and how we uplift greatness in others, creating a torch worth passing and a lasting leadership legacy. That's influence in action!

About The Author

Amber R. Carlson is an eternal student of how our brains learn and our hearts connect. She holds a B.A. in World Religious Studies, an M.S. in Organizational Development and Leadership, and an honorary PhD in Psychology, blending curiosity about what people believe with expertise in how people grow and change.

As CEO and Founder of ARCHway Learning Solutions, Amber has spent more than a decade helping organizations upskill, reskill, and develop their people. She and her team design award-winning training experiences that combine immersive virtual learning with highly interactive, human-centered workshops. Her work is especially known in healthcare and manufacturing industries, where she helps leaders and teams navigate constant change while staying grounded in compassion, clarity, and accountability.

Amber is the author of the best-selling leadership training book *TORCH: Ignite Teams. Forge Legacy.*, the first in her Ignite Your Legacy series. Through narrative storytelling, reflection, and unique exercises, she invites leaders to see every interaction as a chance to build trust, shape culture, and leave a legacy they're proud of. Her series lays out the foundational and transformational lessons leaders need to guide their teams, lead themselves, and intentionally shape the relationships that sustain them.

Recognized as a Top Learning Experience Evolutionist, a Top Learning Management Systems Solutions Provider, Best Adult Learning Specialist, and Learning and Development Mentor of the Year, she bridges the realities of the frontline with the pressures of the C-suite. In her immersive learning workshops, she harnesses the powers of reflection, competition, creativity, and accountability to design experiences that feel real, relevant, and immediately usable and measurable. She is a sought-after speaker, facilitator, and mentor for executives who want more than "check-the-box" training and want real behavior change and real results.

Beyond the classroom and the page, Amber dedicates her time to creating authentic spaces where leaders can take off their armor, share their hearts, and truly be seen. She creates exclusive rooms where empowered networking and genuine connection replace small talk and surface-level conversation. In these spaces, leaders are invited to be honest about their struggles, bold about their dreams, and accountable for the legacy they're building.

Amber's passion for impact extends well beyond her business. As a mother of two amazing kids, she is fiercely committed to modeling what it looks like to lead with courage, compassion, and curiosity. An aspiring artist, she turns to painting and music as another way to explore stories, emotions, and the colors and harmonies of the human experience. Philanthropy is one of her core values, reflected in her work with Holiday HOOPS and ARTs and in charitable giving circles that support a wide range of causes and communities.

In every role—CEO, creator, connector, mother, mentor—Amber is driven by helping others trade autopilot for intention so the life they're busy building is a legacy worth carrying forward. Amber asks, "You're already leaving a mark. Are you willing to pause long enough to choose what it will be and build it on purpose?"

www.archwaylearningsolutions.com
www.igniteyourlegacyseries.com

CHAPTER TWO

Influence in Action: A Journey of Vision, Resilience, and Reinvention

By Paul J. Simino

Part 1 - Built from Belief / The Rhythm That Raised Me

I may have grown up in Florida, but I've always had a New York state of mind, fast, focused, and wired to build. The first rhythm I learned wasn't a drumline or a deal being closed; it was the hush of a church pew at St. Cecelia Interparochial School in Clearwater, with candle wax in the air and the choir humming behind stained glass. Faith didn't come to me through sermons; it arrived in cadence: stand, kneel, serve. That was the metronome of my childhood, the quiet measure that would one day steady my pulse in rooms filled with pressure and noise.

My mother, Sally, kept that rhythm alive at home. She believed in the power of positive thinking before it became a podcast theme. When life pushed, she'd smile and say, "Alright... what's the solution?" That single question rewired my perspective. Problems weren't threats; they were puzzles. She taught me that possibility often hides inside frustration. I can still see her humming in the kitchen while dinner came together, optimism flowing through her hands like choreography. She was my first example of grace under fire.

My father, Joe, balanced her brightness with calm. He wasn't a preacher, but his faith was steady, an anchor on hard days. He would remind me, *"Remember, son, the sun always shines tomorrow."*

Between them, I learned optimism and patience, momentum and mercy. Sally sealed it by sending me to Catholic schools, where the Jesuits instilled values of thinking for the greater good, precision, discipline, and service into the beat already in my blood. We rose when told to rise, spoke when spoken to, and learned that obedience and excellence were brothers in the same family. Those strict classrooms forged something durable, a belief that work is a form of worship. I didn't realize it then, but that quiet order would become the template for every company I built. By my teenage years, I already wanted to sell something, to move people with words.

I wasn't born into boardrooms. My first real job involved a headset, a phone, and a list of names, telemarketing, the kind of work that interrupts dinner. Each click and hang-up became training in humility and human behavior. I learned that tone could open doors that data never could. Every "no" was rehearsal for the next "yes." It taught me resilience; each hang-up sharpened my understanding of people. I discovered that sales is simply empathy with a goal attached, the art of making someone feel understood before they trust you enough to buy. It was pure training ground.

Five years later, I graduated to **GTE Directories**, selling Yellow Page ads when those books still occupied every kitchen drawer. After nearly three years in corporate America, my experience there provided me with something no classroom could: confidence. Engaging daily with business owners at just 21 years old taught me to see opportunities through their eyes and to speak the language of risk and reward. I learned the importance of professionalism, clear marketing, and showing up with both precision and empathy.

I was pitching ROI to business owners twice my age, focusing on outcomes rather than optics. Corporate life had its cold edges, contracts, policies, politics, and I also discovered what ceilings feel like. Performance doesn't always propel you upward; sometimes, politics keeps you grounded. Yet, I took away the best aspects of my time there, applying what GTE taught me about structure, discipline, and effective marketing as a blueprint for my future ventures. I then infused what corporate America often lacked: soul, warmth, and genuine connection to people.

One night, while staring at my reflection in the car window after yet another unproductive meeting, I uttered a simple prayer: *God, show me what's next.*

That job ignited the spark I needed to build something of my own. What followed was my first test of belief: **American Leads Unlimited (doing business as ALU Promotions)**. In the late '90s, I opened my first timeshare marketing call center. Young and hungry, I had just enough faith in myself to ignore the odds. I rented a small office, hired a handful of people, and began dialing. Within months, I was leading a team that could sell vacation dreams better than anyone in the region. The energy was magnetic; people believed in our vision because I believed in them. I poured everything into those rooms: long nights, tough love, motivation, and mentorship.

Within two years, we expanded to four call centers and over a hundred employees. I was leading teams, creating systems, and learning on the fly how to build culture before I even knew that's what it was called. Every ringing phone felt like progress; every closed deal felt like a small miracle. For the first time in my life, I wasn't just working in someone else's vision, I was living inside my own.

We weren't just selling vacations; we were selling trust in thirty seconds. Scripts transformed into conversations and then into appointments. The rhythm grew louder: phones ringing, laughter between calls, the hum of a company discovering itself. I learned to read a room without seeing it, to coach tone amid chaos, and to meet payroll with prayer.

Then the world changed.
September 11, 2001.

The travel industry collapsed overnight. I walked the call floor, hearing only the hum of fluorescent lights. I learned that leadership isn't just a speech; it's about showing up when the lights go out. We made impossible choices with as much grace as we could muster. My partner and I split amicably, each taking two offices. The silence that followed became a teacher. When the rhythm stops, you must build a new one.

Influence in Action: When a crisis derails the plan, influence transforms into presence, calm decisions, compassionate cuts, and the next clear step.

Closing the ALU offices meant I didn't just lose a business; I lost a rhythm. For weeks, my mornings lacked a pulse, no ringing bell, no laughter from the call floor. It's strange how noise can become a comfort while silence can echo with failure.

I used to drive to the empty parking lot just to sit outside the locked doors. I'd imagine the phones ringing, envision my team back in their chairs, and I'd ask God why He gave me something so wonderful only to take it away. The answer didn't come in words; it came as a nudge: build again, but build differently.

That's when I realized entrepreneurship requires faith. You keep believing even when proof is elusive. It's prayer disguised as persistence. I decided that if I ever built another company, it wouldn't just generate profit;

it would create meaning. I didn't know it then, but that loss was making room for OneSimpleLoan. Sometimes destruction is merely construction in disguise.

I pivoted to **finance**. First, Life and Health Insurance and Variable Annuities. The language was new, and it felt different from selling vacations or advertising space, but the pattern was familiar: listen first, speak with empathy, simplify the complex, connect, clarify, and care. This brief venture led me to a former employee who introduced me to **federal student-loan consolidation**, an emerging field where finance met mercy. One call changed everything. A young veterinarian sobbed on the line, overwhelmed by three hundred thousand dollars of debt. Her tears lingered with me long after we hung up. I thought about the millions like her, people who worked hard, followed the rules, earned degrees, and still found themselves drowning in debt. I realized I wasn't selling money; I was selling relief.

Influence in Action: Pivots stick when anchored in empathy. If you can clearly articulate the human pain, you can build a business that serves rather than sells.

That moment birthed **OneSimpleLoan**. Three employees, two desks, one conviction: finance could serve people instead of trapping them. Within three years, we had one hundred eighty-five employees and more than twelve million in revenue. We weren't chasing numbers; we were pursuing fairness. But fairness has its enemies.

We discovered a rule buried deep in the system, the **single-lender law**, that gave Sallie Mae a stranglehold on the market. If a borrower owed even a single dollar, they owned that borrower's future. Imagine a mortgage or auto loan you couldn't refinance, a credit card you couldn't transfer, a marketplace locked by a single gatekeeper. I couldn't unsee it. So, we fought.

We sued the U.S. Department of Education.

As our case progressed, it brought the issue into the open. The outcome was procedural and political, but the result was tangible: the market shifted, and borrowers regained options. The "single-lender" rule ultimately changed, opening choices for students that hadn't existed before. They finally had options again. It wasn't a clean courtroom victory; it was a catalyst.

The lawsuit transformed more than policy; it transformed me. OneSimpleLoan had sparked a national conversation. Reporters called daily, cameras crowded the parking lot, and live interviews filled TV and radio. My phone never stopped ringing. Yet, behind the noise was exhaustion. Each day felt like a test of will. At night, I lay awake staring at the ceiling, wondering if I had taken on more than I could bear.

In those quiet hours, I thought of Sally's optimism and my father's calm. I thought about **Francis**, my wife, who stood beside me when the future was shrouded in fog. Her strength never wavered. She reminded me that faith doesn't fade when business falters; it grows stronger in the rebuilding. Her belief steadied me when logic urged me to quit.

Months passed as the case wound through the courts. Then one morning, I received the call: the law had effectively been repealed. Justice Ginsburg had reviewed the case, and rather than let it devolve into a political spectacle, she dismantled it procedurally. Behind closed doors, Sallie Mae and the Department of Education negotiated quietly to avoid losing face. Nobody wanted to appear defeated, so they simply dismantled the law themselves. It was politics in its purest form, deals and dignity dancing together. What mattered most was the outcome: the market reopened, and borrowers could choose again. It wasn't a clean courtroom win, but it was freedom. It proved that persistence can move mountains that money cannot. In the days that followed, my phone became both a lifeline and a leash. Reporters wanted quotes, partners sought clarity, and employees needed direction. Victory doesn't arrive with a manual; it comes with a megaphone and a spotlight.

Influence in Action: Winning publicly requires leading privately. The louder the headlines grow, the more your team needs steadiness, sleep, and early truth.

I remember standing in the office before dawn, the hum of the vending machine the only sound, and feeling how strange it was to be tired amid triumph. We had fought so long for something larger than ourselves, but I was beginning to realize that success is its own form of stewardship. When people start to believe in your fight, you owe them your stamina.

Francis used to tell me to *pause long enough to feel what I'd earned.* I didn't know how. Every time the phone rang, I reached for the next crisis, the next headline, the next decision. We were heroes for a moment, the underdogs who took on Washington, but heroes don't sleep well.

I had employees who sacrificed weekends, friends who stopped calling, and a body fueled by caffeine and cortisol. I told myself I was too busy to rest, too responsible to stop. What I didn't see was that unchecked momentum becomes a habit of avoidance.

One night, after the last call with our PR firm, I sat alone in the conference room, staring at our mission statement on the wall: *"Finance that serves."* I whispered the words and realized that if I didn't start serving myself, the person inside the mission, I might lose the very faith that built it.

When you win a fight like that, you don't celebrate; you exhale. You try to remember how to breathe again. I spent the following months in Washington, D.C., meeting with policymakers and learning how the machine actually worked. I realized staffers often steer the ship more than senators do; the twenty-somethings with clipboards and coffee cups were the real gatekeepers. To be heard, you had to make the complex simple and the human story impossible to ignore.

At sunrise, the dome of the Capitol looked like hope. By afternoon, it resembled heat shimmer. I learned the choreography quickly: flash the badge, clear security, shake hands, and listen more than I talked. Some days, sincerity filled the hallways; other days, it was just theater in business suits.

Late nights belonged to fluorescent lights and black coffee in hotel lobbies. I'd spread out my notes, underline words like choice and freedom, and try to craft sentences that sounded like policy but felt like prayer. One evening, I called Francis from the steps of the Supreme Court, told her I could see the dome glowing through the mist, and she said, "Remember what it cost you to get here. Don't let the win cost you more." The next morning, I returned inside, exhausted but steady. Washington doesn't care how tired you are; it only listens to those who keep showing up.

One day, on our way to meet a congressman, I was with three other CEOs when the elevator doors opened. Stepping in was **then-Senator Barack** Obama, returning from a cigarette break. You could feel the shift in the air the moment he entered; he carried calm like armor. Henry, one of the other executives, began introducing us and explaining our purpose. Obama listened intently, nodding slightly as we presented our case for fair access in lending. When he looked directly at me, he smiled.

"You're the loan guy, right?"

I laughed. "Trying to make it simple, sir."

He nodded again. "That's how change starts."

He handed us his card and suggested we follow up with his chief of staff. We never secured that meeting, but that brief moment between floors stayed with me. I realized that influence isn't about titles or power; it's about presence. We met with congressmen, senators, and lobbyists, sitting across from people whose signatures could shift national policy.

Not every conversation in D.C. felt that inspiring. One meeting with **Congressman George** Miller, chairman of the Education and Workforce Committee, offered me the straightest talk I ever received in politics. We sat with him for thirty minutes, laying out everything, policy, people, unintended consequences. He listened closely, then said quietly, *"There's a target on your back. Change is coming. Move, or it will move you."* I respected him more for that honesty than for any handshake I ever received.

I took the warning as it was, truth without malice. That same day, I called my forty marketing partners across the country. "We pivot today," I told them. Leadership sometimes means making a decision before the ground has even finished shifting beneath your feet.

During that same round of lobbying, I met with several members of Congress, including **Debbie Wasserman** Schultz. She was sharp, direct, and genuinely interested in understanding how the single-lender rule was affecting real borrowers. Those briefings taught me that influence isn't about party lines; it's about persistence and clarity. If you can explain the human cost, you can reach anyone on either side of the aisle.

Soon after, the power dynamic in Washington shifted, and the student-loan ecosystem transformed with it. A new administration and congressional leadership took office, restructuring the federal lending model, moving more of the market under direct government control and removing many third-party lenders from the process. I'd seen versions of this before: when funding tightens or risk spikes, policy often centralizes to stabilize the system. But centralization always creates winners and losers, forcing a hard leadership truth on me: if your industry depends on regulation, your strategy must include policy risk as a standing line item, not an afterthought.

That shift reminded me how fragile any industry can be when policy changes faster than people can pivot.

Content note: the next section references workplace sexual harassment. A CEO shared with me an inappropriate "condition" implied for a meeting. It reminded me that policy can shift faster than culture, and integrity is a boundary, not a slogan.

During those same months, I heard a story directly from another CEO, someone I had known and done business with for years—that illustrated how old Washington still operated beneath its polished speeches. She had scheduled a meeting with Senator Ted Kennedy's office to discuss proposed changes. When she called to confirm, his chief of staff told her there was a "requirement" for attendance: she should wear something short, black, and tight. Hearing this straight from her made my stomach turn. It was disgusting but not surprising. D.C. had always been a blend of reform and ego. That moment made me realize that changing laws was far easier than changing culture.

After Washington, the power structure shifted again, and I refused to wait for permission to exist. I transitioned into the **private student-loan** marketplace, partnering with major banks like Chase, SunTrust, Discover, and Lehman Brothers. For a while, it worked. We built new marketing networks and helped families refinance outside the federal maze.

Then came the tremor I couldn't ignore. One morning, I turned on the television to see **Dick** Fuld, chairman of **Lehman** Brothers, sitting under the bright lights of a congressional hearing, answering for the collapse of his empire. By that afternoon, Lehman was gone. A company worth $600 billion had evaporated. I stared at the screen, feeling the weight of it. If giants could fall that fast, no one was safe. The recession rolled through like a slow-motion earthquake. Partners vanished. Credit lines froze. The same papers that once celebrated our victory now chronicled another collapse. But this time, I didn't panic. I prayed, listened, and began planning for the next rhythm.

Influence in Action: When giants fall, drift becomes deadly. Your job is to choose a posture quickly, protect cash, protect people, and commit to the next rhythm.

Section 4 – The Sculley Season

In the midst of that economic chaos, another door opened. A connection introduced me to **John** Sculley, the former CEO of **Pepsi** and Apple. His partner, **David A.** Steinberg, had been following our work, and together they wanted to acquire OneSimpleLoan. We spoke for hours about leadership, innovation, and culture. David, John's protégé, was polished and persuasive, a visionary with a knack for spotting potential. I respected his insights and agreed to the sale.

For a while, it felt like validation, proof that what we had built truly mattered. But as the months passed, I learned one of the hardest lessons of my career: when you let someone else steer the ship, even a legend, you risk losing the rhythm that made it float in the first place. Corporate polish can scrape the soul right out of a founder's mission.

That season taught me more than any victory ever could. I learned that you can rent capital, but you cannot rent culture. You can share equity, but not purpose. When the time came, I stepped away with gratitude for the experience and a vow never to forget who I was building for. From that ending emerged the clarity for my next beginning. For the first time in years, my calendar was empty, no calls, no contracts, no morning rush. The silence felt foreign, almost loud. I didn't know how to be still. Francis noticed before I did. She'd prepare a meal for me and say, *"You don't have to rush the next thing. Let it find you."*

At first, I tried to ignore the stillness. I filled my days with errands, reorganized old files, and even alphabetized my bookshelf. But beneath the noise of busywork, there was a hum, that familiar rhythm, soft yet steady, asking, *What's next?*

Weeks later, I found myself writing again. Not business plans, but reflections, paragraphs about purpose, faith, and redemption. I wrote about the people we'd helped, the broken system we'd fought, and how the same knowledge that saved someone's finances might one day save their life.

Francis read one of those pages and said quietly, *"You're not done teaching. You're just changing classrooms."* That line resonated deeply. That night, I opened a fresh notebook and wrote a single phrase across the top: **Education as redemption.**

I remember standing in my office late one evening, fluorescent lights humming, papers stacked like tiny towers of faith. Everything looked the same, yet nothing was the same. In that silence, I whispered the question that would start the next chapter of my life: *What if money isn't the only thing we can help people rebuild?*

If lending could fail, perhaps learning could heal. That thought became my new north star.

I prayed and wrote ideas on yellow pads until the ink bled through. I spoke with my wife, Francis, about what mattered more than margins, purpose. She listened the way she always did, steady and sure, reminding me that faith doesn't end where failure begins. Her belief reignited my own.

Faith tested me outside the office too. Marriage, like business, requires grace. Francis and I have walked through seasons of joy and distance. She taught me that love isn't ownership; it's stewardship. I'm not perfect, but I'm present. Each night, I bow my head and thank God for another chance to get it right, with my children, with my work, with myself.

The first seed didn't come from me; it came from Andy. My good friend and colleague called me one afternoon, newly jobless and newly a father of twins. He'd been running bankruptcy counseling for a large credit counseling company in Orlando, and the experience had opened his eyes to how desperately people needed true financial education.

His situation struck a chord. I was seeking a meaningful bridge after closing my last chapter, and Andy's timing felt like providence. We talked for hours about how his work could evolve and how we could build something that taught prevention instead of merely managing crises. That conversation became the blueprint for the **National Financial Literacy Foundation**.

We started small: two desks, two laptops, one mission. Andy contributed his knowledge of credit counseling and curriculum, while I provided capital, entrepreneurial experience, operations, relationships, and structure. Together, we created online courses on budgeting, credit scores, financial literacy, and saving, lessons designed to restore confidence and empower individuals.

As our vision took shape, we recognized the need for a technical mind to help us scale. That's when we reached out to **Erick**, the self-taught wizard Andy had worked with years earlier. He could translate ideas into systems faster than anyone I'd met. Erick built the framework that enabled our courses to exist online, accessible to anyone with a phone or library computer. His quiet brilliance transformed a concept into a living classroom.

The three of us soon realized that financial literacy was only the beginning. From that foundation emerged **Financial Education Services** and eventually **BKClass**, a bankruptcy-counseling platform that helped thousands rebuild from hardship. What began as a phone call from a friend with twins evolved into a movement of education, empathy, and renewal, an unexpected bridge between failure and faith, and the first heartbeat of what would one day become the **North American Learning Institute**.

We didn't measure success in dollars but in lives recalibrated. When the three companies were acquired three years later, I didn't feel like I was cashing out; I felt like I was graduating. The purpose had been fulfilled, and something larger was calling.

It wasn't just business; it was therapy through knowledge. We sold those companies not out of fatigue but fulfillment. They had served their purpose, and it was time for the next movement.

I didn't know then that it would grow into something far beyond finance, a bridge between learning and healing. But I knew this much: God wasn't done writing my story; He had simply changed the chapter heading. I had learned that influence doesn't always come from volume; it comes from the quiet consistency of showing up, in business, in faith, in family. The years behind me had been filled with risk and reward, but what mattered most were the people who chose to believe alongside me. Andy's faith, Erick's precision, Francis's steadiness, each had mirrored something I couldn't see in myself at the time.

In the long pauses between projects, I began to listen to life's smaller cues again: the sound of the coffeemaker before sunrise, the click of keys on my laptop as I outlined new ideas, and the echo of laughter from my children drifting down the hallway. These sounds reminded me that success isn't a destination; it's the rhythm you create while moving toward purpose.

Looking back, every pivot had been preparation. The call center grind taught me empathy, the years in finance instilled discipline, the lawsuit imparted courage, and Andy's unexpected call, a moment of friendship meeting necessity, taught me to listen for opportunities disguised as needs. I began to understand that the seasons of my life were not scattered events but interconnected verses in a larger song.

The more I reflected, the clearer it became that the next season would focus on scale, not just in business but in impact. If we could create systems that educated and redeemed one person at a time, imagine what we could achieve for tens of thousands. This question kept me awake at night, but not with anxiety; it felt like anticipation, the same energy that hums before the first note of a familiar song.

One night, I wrote in my journal: *Build something that outlives you.* It wasn't about legacy in an ego-driven sense; it was about stewardship. I wanted to transform experience into infrastructure and resilience into reach. The companies I had built were vehicles, but the real destination was transformation, giving others the tools to rewrite their own stories as I had been allowed to rewrite mine. Because influence isn't about what you've achieved; it's about what you continue to give. It's the unseen ripple that follows the stone disappearing beneath the surface.

This realization became the heartbeat that carried me forward. The purpose of every failure was suddenly clear: each setback had been a rehearsal for service. In that light, the past wasn't something to overcome; it was something to honor. The rhythm that began in a church pew at St. Cecelia, which carried through boardrooms, courtrooms, and call centers, was still playing, louder now, but steadier.

I didn't know exactly what form the next chapter would take, but I understood the direction. Influence was no longer about headlines or handshakes; it was about systems that healed. The foundation had been built, and the melody was waiting. It was time to step forward again, not to start over, but to continue the song.

The Father

None of my accomplishments compare to this: being a father. Fatherhood taught me the difference between success and stewardship, one is what you build, while the other is what you leave behind in people.

When I met Francis, she already had two children: **Naithen**, four, and **Lilah**, barely two. I didn't see them as hers; I saw them as ours. I legally adopted Naithen, raised them both, and built a home anchored in love, laughter, and structure.

Today, Naithen works alongside me at NALI, disciplined, driven, and evolving into his own leadership. Lilah, kind and compassionate, dedicates her life to caring for children, guided by her heart. And then there's Crystella, my youngest, radiant, curious, creative, my miniature reflection. We raised our family so seamlessly that Crystella didn't realize her siblings had different fathers until she was twelve. That's the power of genuine love.

People often tell me, "You're a good man for taking on another man's children."
But I never viewed it that way. I saw it as simply showing up. Family, to me, isn't about biology; it's about belief.

Legacy

I still find myself on the sidelines of soccer fields on weekends, microphone in hand, watching teamwork unfold under the Florida sun. Every game concludes, but the spirit keeps playing, that's the essence. If I've learned anything, it's this: influence transforms into legacy when you give people a rhythm they can carry forward. To my children, Naithen, Lilah, and Crystella, may you always find your rhythm.

To paraphrase Frank Sinatra, I've been a puppet, a pauper, a pirate, a poet, up and down, over and out, and through it all, the rhythm never stopped. That is what faith sounds like as it matures.

Part 2 - The Calculated Pivot / From Crisis to Culture at Scale

Section 1 – The Aftershock

The next chapter was about scale. We realized that the same structure we used for teaching financial recovery could help people rebuild in every aspect of life. This idea became the **North American Learning Institute**. NALI started small, with a few hand-written courses and approvals earned through persistence. Soon, we were serving courts, workplaces, and schools across the country. Our programs addressed anger management, parenting, domestic violence prevention, and workforce compliance, each offering a second chance in disguise. We built a digital ecosystem long before online learning became essential.

When **COVID-19** struck, the world halted again, but this time we were ready. While others scrambled to adapt, we were already online and accessible. Enrollment doubled, then tripled. I remember one night sitting in my office, illuminated only by the glow of my monitor, watching the live metrics rise. For the first time in decades, I felt pure stillness, not fear, not pressure, just clarity. This is what preparation feels like, years of persistence finally aligning with purpose.

Running NALI demanded every skill I had ever learned: sales, marketing, compliance, technology, and compassion. We built referral partnerships with probation officers, attorneys, and HR directors nationwide. Tens of thousands of agencies now rely on us to serve their clients. We created a partner portal, a 24-hour platform, and a culture that treats every learner like family. But the measure of success was never profit; it was rhythm, the rhythm of people rising again after a fall.

The lesson was clear: people didn't just need financial literacy; they needed life literacy. They required practical tools for every aspect of rebuilding. I carried that realization into my next endeavor: the **North American Learning Institute**.

Section 2 – Building the Bridge from Finance to Education

Education wasn't merely a business; it was a ministry in disguise. We had witnessed how teaching financial literacy could transform lives, prompting us to ask the same question that had guided our previous major decisions: *what's next?*

The answer emerged gradually, through late-night conversations and notes scribbled on coffee-stained paper. If financial literacy could liberate individuals from debt, what could life literacy accomplish for those trapped in other struggles? Together, we began outlining a vision for something greater: a network designed to teach accountability, communication, empathy, and leadership, a school for second chances.

Andy and I shared this conviction, and **Erick** joined us from the start. He had already contributed to NFLF, FES, and BKClass, quietly building the systems that sustained those programs. As the vision for NALI took shape, his role became even more crucial. We dubbed him *The Wizard* for his ability to create something from nothing. He bridged our ideas with the digital world that could bring them to life. The three of us formed the foundation of what would soon be known as the **North American Learning Institute**.

It began like all great endeavors: small, uncertain, but filled with belief. We crafted our first courses by hand and built our initial website from scratch. A few approvals trickled in from judges and workforce administrators willing to give us a chance. Our earliest programs focused on practical issues: anger management, parenting, domestic violence prevention, and workplace professionalism. Simple topics with significant impact. We aimed to help people rebuild what life had broken.

In those early months, we encountered setbacks that could have derailed most startups. Funding was tight, approvals slow, and technology evolved faster than we could keep up. Yet every small victory, one court approval here, one grateful student there, reminded us that our mission was worth the struggle. Faith filled the gaps that budgets couldn't cover.

We built everything ourselves. **Erick** managed the technology like a composer crafting music only he could hear. **Andy** oversaw the curriculum, compliance, approvals, and marketing, ensuring that every component met the highest standards of quality and integrity. I focused on operations, communications, partner relationships, trademark compliance, and, most importantly, the people involved. Every employee mattered to me. I made it a priority to listen, mentor, and ensure every voice felt valued. In many ways, I became the connective tissue that kept the organization aligned, protected, and human. The three of us met nearly every morning to discuss ideas, challenges, and prayers for clarity. We believed that if we stayed aligned in purpose, everything else would follow.

Bit by bit, it happened. Courts began approving our courses, followed by probation departments and corporations seeking real-world training. Our programs expanded beyond compliance into wellness and workforce development. We aimed for every course to feel personal, not punitive. Each lesson, even when mandated by a judge or employer, carried an undertone of redemption, the belief that everyone deserves a path back.

We didn't spend much on marketing. Our students became our advocates. Upon completing a course, they shared their experience with friends, coworkers, and probation officers. The network grew organically, rooted in trust. By 2018, we had over thirty courses available online in English and Spanish, accepted in nearly every state and Canadian province. The platform wasn't fancy; it was effective. People could log in from a phone, a library computer, or a halfway house and receive the same quality education as anyone else. Dignity in access, that was our promise.

Erick's code held the system together. We joked that he never slept. He could transform an idea scribbled on a napkin into a live feature overnight. That's why we called him *The Wizard*. The three of us met nearly every morning, discussing ideas, challenges, and prayers for clarity. We believed that if we stayed aligned in purpose, everything else would follow.

The North American Learning Institute had become a national presence. We established **relationships** with state agencies, garnered referrals from major employers, and built a growing list of schools using our programs. Yet, despite the momentum, our mission remained unchanged, teach, uplift, redeem. That's when the next storm hit, one that would test every line of code and every ounce of faith we had built together.

Section 3 – The Pandemic Pivot

When COVID arrived, the world stopped overnight. Courthouses closed. Offices went dark. Schools shifted to remote learning. The same silence I felt on September 11 returned, but this time it brought opportunity instead of fear. While others scrambled to transition online, we were already prepared. The foundation we had laid years earlier became a lifeline for thousands of organizations across the country.

Influence in Action: Preparedness is influence in advance. What you build quietly becomes what saves people loudly when the world shifts overnight.

The calls began within days. Probation departments, attorneys, courts, HR managers, and school administrators all inquired if we could accommodate the sudden surge of online students. We didn't hesitate. **I reorganized the** team, Erick scaled the servers, and Andy managed the online marketing efforts. We weren't just keeping a business alive; we were ensuring education remained accessible when people needed it most.

One night during those first chaotic weeks, I sat alone in the office watching our dashboard light up. Students logged in from every state, completing courses that would keep them compliant, employed, or simply grounded during the uncertainty. The glow from the screens filled the room, and I whispered, *this is what purpose looks like when it grows up.*

Our enrollment multiplied almost overnight. What could have broken us became our catalyst. NALI transformed from a modest education company into a national leader. We doubled our staff, refined our technology, and built enduring partnerships. Yet through it all, the most important lesson wasn't about scalability; it was about stewardship. Success means nothing if you forget why you started.

Faith remained my compass. Even as the world tried to define "essential work," I knew ours was exactly that. Education is essential. Dignity is essential. Redemption is essential. Each certificate we issued became more than a piece of paper; it represented proof that someone had completed their course and taken a step toward rebuilding their life.

Francis stayed by my side throughout this journey. She witnessed the long nights, the endless phone calls, and the pressure to keep everything moving. Her calmness became my shelter. She reminded me to breathe, to pray, and to see the people behind the numbers. Her belief made me a better man, and I still thank God for that.

Legacy and the Rhythm Forward

The years that followed focused on refinement, turning growth into grace. My three children, **Naithen, Lilah, and Crystella**, each contributed a unique note to the rhythm of our family. Naithen joined the company, learning every layer of NALI from the ground up. He possesses a mind for strategy and a heart for people, a combination that reflects the best parts of everyone who built this place. Lilah continued on her own path, caring for children and families, pouring her compassion into everything she does. Crystella blossomed into an entrepreneur at heart, fearless, creative, and endlessly curious. Watching her inspires belief in the next generation of builders.

I often think about the faces behind the statistics: the single mother finishing her class after midnight, the veteran rebuilding his career, the teenager learning accountability instead of punishment. They are the reason this work endures. Every story is a verse in the larger song of redemption that NALI continues to write each day.

Looking back now, I see every setback for what it truly was, a setup for the next act. The times I thought I was being broken were simply moments of reshaping. The 9/11 silence, the D.C. battles, the Lehman collapse, the pandemic, each refined my rhythm and deepened the music.

Life, like soccer, is about momentum and heart. You fall, you rise, and you keep the ball moving forward.

I've built and sold companies, but more importantly, I've built people. Andy, Erick, and Francis each carried a piece of the rhythm that made NALI possible. The students who log in every day to rebuild their lives are proof that the work still matters. My children carry that same rhythm in their own ways, and that is legacy enough for me.

We scaled responsibly, maintained quality, and preserved the human connection: courses that help individuals reset their trajectory, satisfy mandates, keep jobs, and rebuild lives. Today, the North American Learning Institute serves courts, Fortune 500 companies, and schools nationwide. It resembles education, but the heartbeat lies in outcomes, reduced recidivism, safer workplaces, stronger families, and a second chance with support.

What does influence in action mean to me? It is not a TED-talk veneer or a viral clip. It is a disciplined pattern: see clearly, decide cleanly, and move fully. Influence isn't granted by title; it is earned through decisions that absorb risk, allowing others to maintain their footing. It manifests in policy work when a monopoly harms the many, in the candid phone call to a partner when the tides are shifting, and in communicating the truth to your team early and often. When favorable conditions finally arise, it involves refusing to get sloppy, protecting the product, maintaining service levels, and preserving the brand's essence as you scale.

If you zoom out, each of these seasons was a classroom, some loud, some brutal, some holy in disguise. I didn't just survive them; I began to recognize the underlying operating system, the decisions that kept the mission human and the outcomes tangible. Before we proceed, here are the principles I've consistently revisited, not theoretical concepts, but scar tissue transformed into structure.

Here are the principles I return to, the operating system beneath the pivots:

1. **Build on First Principles, Not Fads.** Fads implode; principles compound. First principles are the non-negotiables against which you test every decision. For us, these are: (a) measurable outcomes for the learner; (b) frictionless access (mobile, clear UX, fast credentialing); (c) institutional trust (approvals, audits, data hygiene). If a new idea enhances these three, I'm listening. If it doesn't, it's mere seduction, not strategy.

Try this: Write down your top 3 non-negotiables and reject (or pause) any initiative that doesn't reinforce them.

2. **Choose Payroll Courage.** There are moments when being right can jeopardize your company. When Chairman Miller shared the weather report, I faced two choices: defend a narrative or advocate for my team. We made responsible cuts, redeployed talent, and lived to build another day. Courage is rarely cinematic; often, it manifests as spreadsheets at 2 a.m. and a list of names you refuse to let down.

Try this: Identify your "non-negotiable payroll threshold" (runway + headcount) and pre-plan the first two cuts you'd make with dignity.

3. **Tell the Market the Truth...Simply.** Whether I'm briefing a staffer, a judge, or a probation officer, I recognize that attention is scarce.

Remove jargon. Identify the pain. Quantify the gain. Achieve 24 on-time payments, lower your rate by a point. Complete this course to keep your job. Take this training to measurably reduce incidents quarter over quarter. Precision is a gift; simplicity is a megaphone.

Try this: Take your most important message (to customers, staff, or stakeholders) and condense it into a one-page brief: one clear pain statement, one concrete outcome with a measurable metric, and one next step. Then test it on three people outside your bubble, if they can't repeat it back in 10 seconds, cut more jargon and revise.

4. **Own the Culture Levers.** You can rent capital, but you cannot rent culture. If I could do it again, I'd embed the essence into the agreement. I'd safeguard decision rights regarding the customer promise, the hiring standards, and the mission language because these three elements shape outcomes long after the ink dries. Capital accelerates whatever you already are. If you neglect the culture levers, you don't just sell equity, you sell the future.

   If you surrender product quality, hiring standards, and the customer promise to outside interests, you've already sold the company in the most meaningful ways. Partnerships are powerful, but only if your non-negotiables are firmly established.

Try this: Identify your three culture levers (quality, hiring standards, customer promise) and define one decision right you will never relinquish.

5. **Iterate with Dignity.** We build for people facing fragile moments, divorce, probation, employment risk. Our copy, UX, and support scripts must treat learners as adults with futures, not problems with case numbers. Influence lasts longer when your default setting is respect.

Try this: Audit your top three customer touchpoints and eliminate language that prioritizes compliance over human connection.

6. **Keep a Real-World Feedback Loop.** The field beats the deck. Talk to judges who assign your courses. Ask HR directors what truly reduces incidents. Call school counselors about the language that keeps teens engaged. Then implement changes weekly. Influence is not merely the power to speak; it is the humility to listen and the agility to improve.

Try this: Schedule three 15-minute calls with frontline stakeholders and implement one improvement within seven days.

7. **Practice the Calculated Pivot.** Pivots aren't abrupt shifts; they are sequenced decisions made under uncertainty. When shocks occur, be they policy, economic, or viral, you can choose to deny, delay, or decide. Decide. Establish guardrails: cash burn, team thresholds, and customer promises you will uphold. Then act. The market punishes indecision.

Try this: Write your pivot guardrails (cash burn limit, team threshold, customer promise you won't break) and rehearse the first three steps.

8. **Keep One Hand in the Community.** For me, it's soccer, board service, announcing charity matches, helping youth programs elevate their standards. The field reminds me why we build talent pipelines in the first place: people, families, neighborhoods. Influence that doesn't serve the real world is just branding.

Try this: Commit to one recurring community engagement (monthly) that connects you with the individuals your outcomes affect.

9. **Bet on Integrity at Scale.** As I grow older, I increasingly value the power of boring excellence. Approvals are up-to-date, certificates are delivered instantly, and refunds don't devolve into hostage negotiations.

Data is securely stored where it belongs, encrypted as necessary. Scale isn't a staircase of hacks; it's a cathedral of habits.

Try this: Choose one "boring excellence" metric (refund speed, certificate time, audit readiness) and publish it internally every week.

10. **Write It Down.** Memory is a leaky bucket. Influence becomes legacy when you document your journey, lessons learned, scars earned, moments of grace. If you don't write, the next generation will repeat avoidable mistakes. If you do, they'll replicate your best moves more quickly. This book, for me, is a commitment to document it all.

Try this: Create a "Legacy Doc" and add one page: the decision you made, its cost, what it taught you, and what you would do again.

A final word on timing. I've experienced both luck and misfortune in equal measure. I chose travel before 9/11, private lending before the Great Recession, and distance learning before a global lockdown. Two of those choices could have derailed me; one propelled us forward. The constant isn't foresight; it's posture. Keep your head up, your feet moving, and your values fixed. When the ground shifts, influence is the quiet you bring into the room and the clarity you leave behind.

If you're reading this as a CEO, founder, operator, or ambitious contributor, here's my invitation: lead with clear decisions, protect your people early, and make your influence measurable in someone else's life. Drop an interest rate. Save a job. Keep a family intact. Teach a teen on an Xbox. Entrepreneurship isn't a highlight reel; it's a series of stewardship moments woven together by grit, grace, and good humor. Do this long enough, and you'll wake up one day to find that the influence you practiced in private has become the impact others can feel in public.

Through every storm, one truth remains constant: faith is rhythm. You don't need to see the end of the song to trust the beat. I have been tested, refined, and renewed. And if there's one message I want to leave behind, it's this:

I am the storm that builds, not breaks.

About the Author

Paul J. Simino is a visionary entrepreneur, CEO, and mentor whose career spans more than three decades across business, education, and social impact. A New York native raised in Florida, Paul has spent his life turning challenges into opportunities and ideas into movements.

As the founder of **OneSimpleLoan**, Paul led the company that became a catalyst for repealing the federal *Single Lender Law*, opening the student-loan market to true competition and freedom of choice for millions of borrowers nationwide. His bold leadership earned him national recognition in *The Washington Times*, *Florida Trend*, and *The Tampa Bay Business Journal*, along with coverage in numerous financial and education media outlets.

After a successful exit from the finance world, Paul channeled his passion for service into education, co-founding the **National Financial Literacy Foundation (NFLF)** and **Financial Education Services (FES)** with his longtime colleague and friend, Andy. Together with their technical partner, Erick — known affectionately as "The Wizard" — they built **BKClass.com**, a bankruptcy-counseling platform that has helped thousands rebuild from financial hardship.

Today, as the CEO of the **North American Learning Institute (NALI)**, Paul leads one of the nation's most respected online education organizations, providing court, workplace, and personal development programs to hundreds of thousands across North America. His work blends innovation, empathy, and accessibility, proving that technology can be a tool for redemption as much as for efficiency.

Beyond business, Paul is a devoted father, faith-driven leader, and lifelong soccer enthusiast. Whether speaking to executives, mentoring young entrepreneurs, or announcing from the sidelines of a youth match under the Florida sun, he embodies the same rhythm that has guided his life: **discipline, compassion, and courage in action.**

Paul's philosophy is simple: *Influence isn't about power — it's about presence.* His journey, from telemarketer to national changemaker, stands as living proof that faith, resilience, and vision can transform both lives and systems.

Media Mentions & Press Highlights

Tampa Bay Times — *Oldsmar man leads student loan fight* *Feature profile on Paul Simino's landmark lawsuit challenging U.S. Department of Education policy and reshaping the student loan industry.*

The Chronicle of Higher Education — *Student lender loses a lawsuit, loses critical business, and sees victory* *Analysis of OneSimpleLoan's legal battle and its broader impact on higher education lending practices.*

Tampa Bay Business Journal — *Small Business of the Year Recognizing OneSimpleLoan's rapid national growth and Paul Simino's leadership as a Florida entrepreneur.*

PRWeb — *OneSimpleLoan Honored by Upper Tampa Bay Chamber of Commerce Press release celebrating Business of the Year award and industry recognition for innovation in financial services.*

College Recruiter Blog — *Will a lawsuit resuscitate reconsolidation of student loans? Coverage of the OneSimpleLoan case and its implications for student borrowers nationwide.*

FindLaw — *U.S. 2nd Circuit: OneSimpleLoan v. U.S. Dept. of Education Official federal case record documenting the landmark challenge that led to repeal of the "single lender rule."*

U.S. Department of Justice — *OneSimpleLoan v. Spellings (Opposition Brief) Official Supreme Court filing detailing the Department of Education's response in the historic case.*

Florida Trend Magazine — *Top Florida Entrepreneurs to Watch Recognized among Florida's innovative business leaders shaping finance and education policy.*

College Recruiter Blog — *Paul Simino of OneSimpleLoan Honored by Ernst & Young Coverage of Simino's nomination as an Ernst & Young Entrepreneur of the Year finalist in Florida.*

EzineArticles — *Paul Simino – Expert Author Profile Published thought leadership on entrepreneurship, financial literacy, and organizational growth.*

CHAPTER THREE

Perseverance

By Joseph Iturria

Depending on the study and the industry, many new businesses fail to survive past the five-year mark. The exact number varies. I'm not here to debate percentages; my goal is to ensure that you and I don't become one of them.

I strongly believe in anomalies, the outliers. In business, an anomaly is the leader who persists even when data suggests they should quit. Often, what distinguishes that person from others isn't luck; it's perseverance.

Consider companies like Airbnb, Tesla, SpaceX, Pinterest, Facebook, and Stripe, each seemed impossible at the outset. Yet, their leaders shared a common trait: they continued to build despite resistance. That's perseverance.

Endurance is the ability to withstand a setback and remain standing. Perseverance, on the other hand, is the ability to take that setback and continue moving toward the goal. If you want to lead people and have real influence, you must not only survive obstacles; you must navigate through them. When you combine vision with endurance, you create perseverance. It's like hiking through a storm; you don't stop just because the wind howls. You keep moving because you can see the trail marker, know the route, and trust there's a way through. That's leadership: you forge ahead because you can envision where you're guiding others.

Regardless of your faith background, the principle remains: people progress when they have direction—and leaders persevere when they can see beyond the storm. Think of Moses, who led a nation through the wilderness; he persevered because he had a clear destination. Great strategists endure battles because they see a path to victory.

Everyone faces obstacles. If you're a CEO, you can expect challenges, mountains, and hurdles.

It is during these challenges, both mountains and valleys, that the quality of perseverance becomes essential. The ability to envision the other side is a rare but vital skill.

I remember when we secured our first large commercial contract. I bid on the project without the necessary funds to begin, but I knew our vision was greater than our current situation. When the call came that we were awarded the project, anxiety set in: This is too big. We can't manage this.

We lack resources. But the end goal was clear. I understood we needed to tackle that mountain.

The immediate obstacle was financial. After taking a day to think it through, I found a creative way to raise the necessary funds. By the next day, we had what we needed, and I could confidently say yes.

That's perseverance: fear may arise, but vision remains stronger. You must understand that growth requires discomfort, necessitating strategic moves and difficult decisions to advance the business. This is part of persevering.

In 2023, I undertook another project that cost over a hundred thousand dollars to complete. I effectively paid that amount out of pocket due to a miscalculation in the bidding process. This was another pivotal moment where I could have chosen to give up and succumb to despair. Thankfully, through prayer, a creative idea emerged for attracting new business. Within months, I generated enough profit to recover the funds lost. There are countless moments I could discuss, from financial complexities to staff changes and tough clients; anyone who has been in business long enough can relate, and I hope this resonates with you. You are not alone in this journey, persevere and keep your eyes on the end goal. Looking back, perseverance wasn't simply about staying positive; it was about taking responsibility under pressure. It taught me to refine my processes: I altered how we review bids, calculate risk, and protect margins to avoid repeating the same mistake. Perseverance isn't denial; it's ownership combined with forward momentum.

As you pursue your goals, consider what sets you apart in your industry. How do you perceive and tackle problems as they arise? Do you view challenges as opportunities or as signs of impending doom?

As humans, we often allow past experiences to shape our responses to crises, which in turn affects our influence within our organization, the team we manage, and our engagement with clients. Think of Joseph from the Bible, betrayed by his brothers, sold into slavery, and imprisoned. He epitomizes perseverance. His gifts ultimately allowed him to rule Egypt and become a successful businessman. When famine loomed, he didn't panic; he prepared. When sold into slavery, he earned his master's trust. Even in prison, he gained the warden's confidence. Each betrayal and obstacle didn't hinder his mindset; he pushed through and thrived. In fact, it was his influence in prison that led to his release.

Perseverance will help you view challenges as opportunities that propel you toward your next milestone.

You cannot be paralyzed by fear; you must change how you perceive challenges. When faced with a challenge, ask yourself:

1. Why did this happen?
2. Did I allow this, directly or indirectly? What can I change right now to prevent it from happening again?
3. Did my initial reaction improve or worsen the situation?
4. What are three creative solutions I can test immediately?
5. What is the end goal, and what steps can I take by working backward from it?

Perseverance will grant you the perspective needed to see challenges clearly.

Perseverance will keep you *moving forward.*

Perseverance shapes how you respond to challenges and influences your reactions under pressure. Your response affects your influence, which in turn shapes your organization's culture. This culture impacts outcomes: how your team performs, how they treat customers, and whether the organization grows stronger or begins to fracture.

In the midst of a battle, your ability to persevere will translate into your bottom line. For example, when faced with an upset customer, will you convey fear or anger to your team? Or will you maintain focus on the end goal, endure the pain caused to the company, and share a vision with your team to mitigate future problems by avoiding the same mistakes?

When experiencing a financial crisis, will you throw your hands up in defeat, or will you believe in your vision enough to endure the financial strain and find a way out? Perseverance enables you to absorb the impact, keeping your team steady and allowing them to push forward!

Influence comes with vision. When your team can see and feel the vision, they will strive to overcome problems and achieve victory. This is perseverance.

With perseverance comes influence. Influence attracts people who rally around your vision to help you achieve your goals.

Here's the truth: you can persevere personally, but you need a team to push through collectively. In my business, I live by one motto: **make allies, not enemies.** It's easy to respond with anger, blame others, or walk away. But leadership is about guiding people to move together toward a common goal, even in the face of real obstacles.

In leadership, the art lies not in how hard you can attack, but in your ability to inspire a group to work collaboratively and advance toward a shared objective despite challenges.

True leaders possess influence and leverage it to unite people toward a common goal. The essential ingredient in achieving this is perseverance.

Here are a few key takeaways to effectively influence your team during adversity:

1. **Lead with vision, not fear.** When adversity strikes, respond with a strategy for moving forward. Your vision serves as your anchor. Communicate it clearly to your team: "Here's the goal, here's what we know, and here's our next move."

2. **Become a problem solver intentionally.** Businesses exist to solve problems. Train yourself to seek solutions, not assign blame. Ask, "What does the customer need, and how can we deliver it better?"

3. **Pause before you speak in high-pressure situations.** If you're unsure of what to say, take a moment. Walk, read, or disconnect before responding. Your calm demeanor protects your influence.

4. **Don't go it alone.** You need your team, and they need you to remain steady. Collaborate with individuals who excel in key areas, and rely on their strengths when challenges arise.

About the Author

Joseph is the CEO and founder of Renew, a company he established in 2011 with a vision for integrity, excellence, and craftsmanship. Under his leadership, Renew has grown into a trusted name, known for its commitment to quality work and genuine care for clients and communities alike.

With a strong work ethic and a heart for people, Joseph leads with humility and purpose. He believes in building not only structures, but long-lasting relationships, ensuring that every project reflects his values of honesty and dedication.

Beyond his professional accomplishments, Joseph is a devoted husband and family man. He approaches every part of his life with the same steady character and warmth that have shaped his company's success. He continues to guide Renew with a passion for creating, serving, and making a meaningful impact.

CHAPTER FOUR

From A Single Thought to a System of Impact and Legacy

By Loreta Tarozaite

At ten years old, I sat on the carpet of our small apartment in Lithuania, glued to the flickering light of the TV as my family watched prime-time news. The anchor, composed and powerful, sat behind her desk.

"One day I will be doing this."

We lived under the shadow of the Soviet Union, with closed borders and restricted voices. Most people kept their dreams to themselves, afraid to want too much.

Yet, the thought lingered. I didn't contemplate how or when; I just believed my future as a news anchor awaited me.

Years later, my father bought and installed a satellite dish, an exciting and costly addition at the time. For the first time, we could access programs from beyond our borders.

That's when America appeared: bright colors, fast talkers, open roads, and a language that felt alive.

"I want to go to America."

With the collapse of the Soviet Union, new opportunities emerged. I applied for a student exchange program, which required passing an English-language SAT and an interview with Americans. It was exhilarating to engage with native English speakers.

Once accepted, I was assigned to Texas. It was an interesting and transformative year for my developing teenage mind. I hadn't anticipated the prevalence of country music, cowboy hats, and church.

However, other aspects of America were precisely what I had envisioned. I felt possibility everywhere. Back home, people spoke of America as the land of dreams, a place where you could become anyone, where ideas could flourish, and where limits didn't confine you.

In other words, I caught the "American Dream" bug.

I didn't realize it at the time, but this is how my life unfolded: a thought would arise, I would pursue it, and the next environment would shape the next version of me.

"I want to realize myself professionally and become an entrepreneur."

In 1995, I began attending Vilnius University in Lithuania, studying journalism with a focus on broadcast. During my final year, one of my professors, a prime-time news anchor, asked if I'd be interested in auditioning for a business news program.

On audition day, I was placed immediately in front of the camera. I read the teleprompter and secured the job on the spot.

Several years later, I became one of the youngest prime-time news anchors in Lithuania. Suddenly, I found myself sitting behind the very same desk I once saw on that flickering screen.

The best part? I discovered I was a natural in the newsroom. I worked quickly and stayed organized. The late-night news was ready before I left the prime-time evening show, and morning segments were mapped out, allowing me to focus solely on overnight changes.

Most importantly, that newsroom became my first systems lab. Producers, reporters, camera operators, and broadcast engineers, all interconnected. Everything had to be in sync; every second counted.

For instance, a news report didn't come together solely because of talent. It materialized through precise handoffs: producer to anchor, anchor to camera, camera to control room, control room to broadcast. If one link faltered, the entire chain collapsed. My first lesson was clear: talent doesn't scale, systems do.

Then everything changed.

I met my partner, who received a job offer in California, the land of Hollywood and innovation.

We moved to Silicon Valley, the epicenter of startups and tech innovation. Google, Apple, Intel, eBay, names I had only heard from a distance, were now just around the corner.

I had finally arrived at the place I had long dreamed of, yet somehow felt invisible. I transitioned from a fast-paced newsroom to a quiet rental apartment.

Without a work visa, I waited nearly three years for the green card that would allow me to pursue my career legally. The days grew quiet, and I felt my identity fading.

Still, I craved stories. I discovered Netflix and became efficient at managing DVD shipments, filling our new home with movie noise to satisfy my visual storytelling cravings.

Years passed, and eventually, I began raising children. My only outings were with other mothers, and our conversations endlessly revolved around playdates and meals.

I called my mother in Lithuania daily and often found myself in tears.

"I need to be seen again."

I enrolled in an online MBA program at the New York Institute of Technology. At the time, I was pregnant and nursing, balancing sleepless nights with business case studies.

In one virtual class, the professor suggested we network on LinkedIn. I had no idea what that meant. As a non-native English speaker, the word "network" conjured images of a spider web.

The challenge wasn't my English; it was my lack of fluency in the *business meaning* of words. Networking was a system of trust, repetition, and access to opportunities. Once I recognized that, I knew I could learn it.

Determined, I went online, typed in "LinkedIn," created an account, and discovered it was a tool for connecting with professionals. It opened my mind to the vast world of business I had yet to understand.

"I want to become a master networker."

While scrubbing the floors one afternoon, I heard an ad for the local Chamber of Commerce. I picked up the phone and called my contact in charge of memberships.

That same week, I attended my first volunteer meeting and was immediately immersed in the business world, where networking came naturally to everyone.

One chamber event led to another. I met individuals from various backgrounds: marketers, entrepreneurs, small business owners, and founders. The more I learned, the more opportunities seemed to arise.

I quickly expanded my reach. I discovered tech meetups and events throughout Silicon Valley, venturing out each week to at least one to connect with new people and gain insights.

Through these connections, I began producing videos for small companies, helping them share their stories. One project led to another, and soon I realized what had happened: I had founded LoretaTV, my own video storytelling business!

The idea I once had in Texas had taken shape. I had become an entrepreneur.

My business had a clear mission: to humanize companies by showcasing the people who drive them forward. It felt reminiscent of broadcasting, but now I was behind the camera, constructing the story rather than merely delivering it.

That's when I discovered my true strength: drawing out people's thoughts and helping them express their messages with confidence. Leaders would give me a five-minute overview, and I would listen, cut through the noise, and surface the essence. "Your key points are here," I'd say. "Say this, phrase it this way, and target this audience."

After years of feeling invisible, I found purpose again by helping others become visible. Information, communication, and words became my craft, and presence became my product.

I didn't have a new spotlight handed to me; I built visibility as a system, intentionally, one connection, one message, and one consistent action at a time.

One contract project brought me to a tech company called ARM. They mentioned they'd hired me because their internal video team wasn't available. Curious, I asked about the "internal team" and learned about in-house work.

I remember thinking how different it must feel to be on the inside, to belong to a company's core. America's corporate culture was still foreign to me, and I wanted in.

"I want to get in-house."

I opened LinkedIn again, started searching, and soon stepped into corporate life. My first job landed me at Sandisk, the company that "killed" the analog film business.

I still remember driving to my first day of work. It was April 1, 2013, ten years after moving to Silicon Valley. I thought to myself, "Can this be real? Did I actually make it? It better not be an April Fool's joke..."

Fortunately, it was not. My role at Sandisk allowed me to see the larger picture of how departments, systems, and leadership work in tandem. I collaborated with the heads of branding, executive communications, marketing, and sales. I could sense how each position connected, and American business began to make sense.

For the first time, I saw the entire system: how decisions are made, how culture impacts execution, how misalignment creates friction, and how communication and cross-functional collaboration build momentum. I realized I could do more than video storytelling; I could naturally integrate all the parts and create the structure.

I envisioned how I would lead, connect people, and establish new processes that truly worked.

"One day, I will run a department."

I immersed myself in digital marketing, PR, and content strategy to understand the full ecosystem and connect its moving parts. Curiosity became my edge, shifting me from storyteller to strategist, from video producer to architect of communication.

Visual storytelling was my starting point, but I quickly expanded beyond it. I was ready to be more than the "Video Queen."

Over time, I began to see the limits of large corporations. I had the knowledge and drive to lead, but the existing structure didn't allow for it. It was time for a new chapter.

"I'm ready to expand my impact."

Michael, the president of Phison's U.S. office and my neighbor at the time, called unexpectedly. He had seen me leading a local media project and believed I could "run marketing communications."

When I joined Phison in 2020, there was no marketing department or structure. The company's leaders wanted visibility in the U.S. but lacked a foundation to support it.

With a shockingly small budget, I built Phison's first corporate marketing function from the ground up, educating the team on what marketing communications truly meant and why it mattered. By 'small,' I mean we had to work smart. Without a big agency safety net, limited tools, and a marketing roadmap that had to prove results quickly.

Unbeknownst to me, I was already constructing the system I had been preparing for my entire career, aligning teams, communication, *and* storytelling.

As results at Phison grew, I became curious about how other leaders transformed their successes into structure. I learned from entrepreneurs I admired and noticed a pattern: they had recognizable and transformational frameworks. They distilled entire processes into just a few words, sometimes even an acronym! It fascinated me.

"I need to create my own framework."

In 2022, I hired a brand consultant to help me gain perspective. Through our work, she reflected back the pattern I had been living all along: People. Process. Presence.

People: who we empower, how we lead, and what we make possible in others.
Process: how work moves clearly, consistently, and without confusion.
Presence: how we show up in the room and in the market, and what people feel when they experience our brand.

For the first time, my entire approach had a language.

It took time for those three words to settle in, and I kept them to myself. For nearly two years, I found myself returning to them, catching myself mid-project and recognizing: this is process, this is people, this is presence.

What I had instinctively done for years now had a structure, and the system began to manifest everywhere: in how I built teams, led meetings, created workflows, and told stories.

At Phison, the impact was clear. Our storytelling grew stronger. Our media coverage increased from 44 stories in 2021 to 368 stories in 2024, reaching 2.48 billion media impressions as recorded through our media monitoring and internal reporting *(Source: MuckRack software for PR teams)*. My 3Ps framework was effective, even though no one in the company knew its name.

However, numbers only told part of the story. What mattered most to me was how people were evolving. How they communicated, how they engaged, and how they embraced the system and structure we were building together. We actively removed silos between teams, supported individual growth, ensured the company presented itself consistently, and built genuine trust with customers.

That's when I realized my work transcended any framework or system. It was not solely about processes or deliverables.

"I want people to feel impacted when they work with me."

In 2024, I asked Phison to support my initiative to bring my expanding, fully remote marketing department together for an in-person offsite to plan for 2025. I wanted everyone to unite, to strategize, and to feel inspired about the year ahead. The idea was approved, and I rolled up my sleeves, ready to drive change and impact.

I opened my PowerPoint template and stared at a blank slide. It was my idea to gather everyone, yet I suddenly felt stuck. How do I lead? How do I inspire belief in the mission I set for my department?

I kept drafting, deleting, and redrafting, but nothing resonated. I spent nights uncertain, wondering what I was missing.

Then, one morning, I woke up with complete clarity. It was the 3Ps, the same People, Process, and Presence framework I already operated within.

That's when I realized that without a framework, leadership devolves into endless drafting. A framework liberates you by providing a pathway to clarity.

I structured the company's goals around the 3Ps and prepared to introduce them to my team.

At the off-site, we aligned, built, and grew. I watched my team learn and fully adopt my 3Ps framework to plan their yearly goals.

One year later, it was time for the second annual team off-site. This year, we included cross-functional teams to extend my framework to other departments.

On the day of the event, the room buzzed with energy. Our expanded team was planning, collaborating, and exchanging ideas for the upcoming year's goals. Everyone spoke the same language, utilized the same 3Ps structure, and embraced the framework I had once only imagined.

I stood quietly for a moment, watching the movement I had initiated. It had all become real.

This was the impact I had always wanted to make, not to be the loudest voice in the room, but to be the one who connected it all. I aimed to help people see what they couldn't yet envision and to build something they could carry forward long after I moved on.

I also felt a wave of unexpected emotion.

The 10-year-old girl watching prime-time TV news.

The young woman behind the anchor desk.

The mother balancing nap times and her own dreams.

Every version of her stood beside me, witnessing her thoughts take form.

Looking back now, none of it feels accidental. Each moment led seamlessly to the next, as if it already knew my destination. Every stage of my life left a trace in the next: the communicator, the mother, the builder, the leader.

I used to think I had to chase what I wanted, but I've learned that everything unfolds when you move with intention and remain open to what calls you.

My life has been a series of quiet thoughts that found their way into the world.

Not forced. Not planned. Just followed.

Today, my thought is, "I want to leave a legacy."

And I can't wait to witness every unexpected way this thought will unfold.

Key Takeaways

1. Every transformation starts with a single idea.

Every major shift in my life began as a thought, not a business plan or a strategy deck, but a spark of belief that something more was possible. Each thought carried momentum because I acted on it, even before knowing where it would lead.

For you: You don't have to chase your dreams. The right opportunities meet you halfway when you lead with clarity and intention. Trust your direction.

2. If you are a professional, your framework already exists.

My 3Ps framework, People, Process, Presence, reflected how I naturally worked and perceived the world. Naming the pattern gave shape to everything I had been doing instinctively.

For you: Your best framework is already in motion. Study how you think, decide, and lead. Then define it clearly so it can guide your team and scale your impact.

3. Visibility is built, not granted.

I went from being seen by millions to feeling invisible in a new country. Rebuilding my career taught me that visibility isn't a spotlight; it's a strategy.

For you: Don't wait to be noticed. Define how you want to be seen, communicate that consistently, and make your presence a measurable part of your leadership.

4. Networking is not a personality trait; it's a practice.

I once believed professional connections developed naturally over time. While this is true, I learned that networking is also a skill built through repetition: intentionally showing up, staying curious, asking questions, following up, and consistently expanding your network.

For you: Don't wait until you feel the moment is right. Build your network systematically, one step at a time.

5. Systems create freedom and sustainability.

The newsroom taught me that alignment drives performance. Every person, every cue, every second mattered because the system enabled precision.

Later, I implemented similar structures within companies. Once people understood what to expect and how their work connected, performance improved naturally. The system fostered clarity and better results.

For you: Build systems that provide your teams with direction, consistency, and space to think. When people grasp the plan, they move faster, communicate more clearly, and show up stronger. Structure isn't a restriction; it's what makes excellence repeatable.

6. Reinvention is a process, not a leap.

Every chapter of my career built on the last: journalism, entrepreneurship, corporate leadership. Nothing was wasted. Reinvention didn't come from starting over; it stemmed from leveraging what I had learned to move forward with greater determination.

For you: Every experience, even those that initially seem like detours, provides valuable data for your next evolution.

7. Align People, Process, and Presence for lasting impact.

The 3Ps weren't invented in a workshop; they evolved through experience. When I introduce this framework to companies, it becomes a shared language that unites teams and builds momentum.

For you: Before adding another tool, AI, or campaign, ask three questions:

- Do we have the right people empowered?
- Do we have a clear process they trust and follow?
- Does our presence reflect who we truly are and where we are going?

When those three align, you gain more visibility, authority, and influence in the market.

A reflection exercise

People: Review the org chart, clarify roles, and map internal communication flows that create bottlenecks and silos between cross-functional and global teams.

Process: Take inventory of the marketing tech stack, review recently missed timelines, and assess what's causing inefficiencies and lack of ownership.

Presence: Conduct a brand audit for messaging and visual storytelling, evaluate leadership's visibility, and assess the customer journey to identify overall consistency in the brand experience.

Action: Choose one of the three areas and implement one visible change within the next 7 days.

How to Reach Loreta

If you're ready to align your people, process, and presence for greater impact, connect with Loreta Tarozaite to begin the conversation. Scan the QR code below and take a 2-minute Brand Presence/Growth Assessment.

📧 : Loreta@loreta.today

🌐 : loreta.today

Scan Me

About the Author

Loreta Tarozaite

Founder and CEO of Loreta Today | Head of Global Corporate Marketing, Phison

B2B leaders reach out to Loreta when they feel stuck. She helps executive teams transition from clutter and friction to clarity and action.

As a Fractional Chief of Staff and CMO, Loreta advises founders and executive leadership teams on addressing issues such as messy communication, disconnected departments, and brand stories that no longer align with the company's direction. Rather than simply providing a plan and disappearing, she embeds herself within the organization, fostering alignment and building the structure that keeps strategy alive.

Her proprietary framework transforms fragmented operations into unified systems that enhance visibility, trust, and growth. Loreta believes that while AI can scale dysfunction, it does not solve it. Therefore, she focuses on strengthening the human and operational foundations that allow technology to deliver real results.

Before stepping into strategic advisory roles, Loreta honed her skills in prime-time news, where she learned to distill complexity into clarity under pressure. This newsroom discipline now informs her leadership style, communication, and ability to help executives present themselves authentically and confidently—whether on camera, on stage, or in the boardroom.

Additionally, Loreta has led global video storytelling for major technology brands, including SanDisk and Western Digital. Currently, she oversees global marketing and communications for Phison, where she built the marketing function from the ground up, launched the enterprise brand Pascari, and introduced its first AI-driven marketing initiatives.

As the founder of Loreta Today, she partners with B2B tech companies and investors, guiding them through growth and transition to realign people, processes, and presence, ensuring the business operates with clarity.

Regardless of where the engagement begins, the outcome remains consistent: sharper alignment, stronger leadership, and a company that functions as well internally as it appears externally.

CHAPTER FIVE

Build the Door, Reinvention, AI, and the Human Capital Lifeline

By Jennifer Sheets

"If opportunity doesn't knock, build a damn door."

Milton Berle said it, but I lived it.

Nothing in my life arrived easily or on schedule. I did not inherit a roadmap; I built one, sometimes out of sheer will, sometimes out of desperation, and sometimes out of faith so thin it felt like breathing through a straw. I imagined my life would unfold very differently. Every pivot, hardship, miracle, and reinvention prepared me for this moment in history, a collision of AI, talent crises, workforce upheaval, and human resilience.

It all started with a leap.

This chapter is about what I learned the hard way: reinvention isn't optional anymore, and AI will either strip the humanity from work or amplify what makes people unstoppable. Your job is to build the door that keeps the human core alive.

From Nothing to Nashville

I did not come to Nashville with a plan. I arrived with a trailer of belongings bungee corded down by my dad and a belief that if I did not create a new life, my old one would consume me. I didn't know a soul and had no money. What I did have was a chance.

Three days after moving into my third-floor walk-up, my car was broken into. Everything of value was gone, especially my mother's wedding ring, tucked in the glovebox. I sat on the apartment floor and cried, asking God if I had made the biggest mistake of my life. Then came that still, undeniable calm: **You are exactly where you are supposed to be.**

Twenty-plus years later, that whisper proved prophetic.

I built a staffing agency from scratch, MasterStaff Inc., and ultimately placed over 40,000 people across various industries. I built a career, a family, and a life. None of it came without brutal chapters.

The truth is: leadership doesn't pause for pain, and systems don't stop just because your heart is breaking.

Life Punches Harder Than Business Ever Could

My son's leukemia diagnosis at three and a half was the first punch.

His relapse was the second.

The third diagnosis and bone marrow transplant were the knockout blows that taught me what survival really is. I was a CEO with a dying child. There is no handbook for that kind of pain, and no playbook for building a business while praying you do not lose your child.

I share this carefully, not for sympathy, but because it taught me what resilience actually costs and what it demands.

But here is the part I am most proud of.

Today, my son is nineteen years old.

He is a sophomore at The Ohio State University, studying aerospace engineering. He is brilliant, determined, compassionate, and living proof that miracles can outlive nightmares.

I also have a beautiful fifteen-year-old daughter who is creative, intuitive, wise beyond her years, and a constant reminder that life can provide soft places to land after seasons that nearly broke you.

Life did not stop during any of this. Bills did not stop. Employees still needed payroll. Clients still demanded talent. I prayed and put one foot in front of the other, surviving the only way you can when there is no option but forward.

Then came the recession, the worst since the Great Depression. I watched the bottom fall out of the staffing world. Companies froze hiring; others collapsed. Everything I had built teetered.

But the hardest moment was not the economy, nor cancer, nor fear.

It was betrayal.

The Vendor Management Extortion, The Moment I Learned What Integrity Costs

A vendor management firm explicitly told me that remaining in the vendor pool required an additional $50,000 payment outside the contract. It was communicated to me as a condition of access, despite the fact that they already received a percentage of invoices. I experienced it as coercive and unethical, and I refused.

Imagine being a single mother with a sick child, a recovering business, and a team depending on you, all threatened by bribery.

I did not have fifty thousand dollars. Even if I had it, my integrity was not for sale.

The consequence was immediate: I was removed from that account. I learned a hard truth: sometimes integrity costs you revenue in the short term... but it saves your soul, your reputation, and your future.

And it was only a matter of time before technology finished what greed started.

Seeing the AI Storm Before It Hit

When COVID arrived, I instantly recognized we were entering what I called the Technology Apocalypse. By 'Technology Apocalypse,' I mean a speed of change so extreme that human systems, hiring, culture, leadership, and even identity struggle to keep up. Overnight, the world digitized. Companies raced to automate, consolidate, and eliminate human touch points. AI moved from a background player to the main act.

Every industry began moving toward:

- One-stop-shop platforms.
- Automated decision making.
- Integrated workflow systems that reduce human handoffs.
- Algorithmic screening that replaced human judgment.

Here is the problem.

You cannot trap human nature like lightning in a bottle.

People are unpredictable. Humans adapt, grow, fail, and reinvent. No algorithm can fully replicate experience, intuition, or character.

The industry chased efficiency at the cost of humanity. Hiring became a wreckage of glitchy job boards, mismatched talent, and broken trust.

That was when I knew my voice was no longer optional.

Finding My Voice and Amplifying It

I wrote my book, Human Capital Lifeline, as a wakeup call for business leaders drowning in noise and starving for clarity. I began speaking nationally, in Chicago, in Rhode Island, and in rooms filled with CEOs watching the same technology tsunami hit their industries. My message was clear.

AI and tech must be integrated responsibly, or we will create the Great Upside Down.

Then came radio.

SuperTalk 99.7 WTN in Nashville offered me a one-hour weekly talk show, Master the Workforce. That show became my platform to educate, challenge, expose, and inspire. It expanded into a podcast with more than two hundred episodes featuring CEOs, athletes, founders, technologists, entertainers, workforce experts, and people who rebuilt after unimaginable adversity.

The power was not fame.

It was truth.

People were not alone. They needed to hear that.

The Workforce Crisis, The Numbers Do Not Lie

The workforce crisis is measurable, and it's showing up on both sides of the table:

- 77% of employers say they can't find the talent they need.
- 72% of candidates say they can't get a human to read their resume.

- A significant share of resumes are filtered out automatically due to formatting or keyword mismatches.
- Some systems have been accused of reinforcing age-related bias, which has become part of ongoing legal and ethical scrutiny.
- Class action lawsuits and regulatory scrutiny have targeted parts of the hiring-tech ecosystem.
- Many companies report that senior roles can take months to fill.

The system is broken on both sides.

AI did not create the fracture; it exposed it by scaling decisions so fast and so wide that every weakness in hiring, leadership, and trust became impossible to hide.

So How Do We Rise

There are three pillars every worker and every leader must master.

One. Pivot Relentlessly

Reinvention is not failure; it's strategy.

If you're over forty, you already know the world will change whether you're ready or not. Your edge is your willingness to evolve without losing your core.

This week: identify one skill you need for the next 18 months and start a learning plan today.

Two. Identify the Market Gaps

Be the human at the helm of your AI tools, not the passenger being replaced by them.

Use AI to sharpen your thinking, speed your execution, and widen your options. But never outsource your judgment, your ethics, or your creativity.

This week: choose one AI tool and build one workflow that saves time without sacrificing quality.

Three. Remember Who You Are

You are the superpower.

Your resilience, instinct, integrity, and creativity are not data points; they're differentiators. Algorithms can screen, but they cannot measure soul.

This week: write a one-paragraph personal value statement that no machine could replicate, and let it guide your next move.

The Human Capital Lifeline and the Future We Are Building

After twenty-five years, the industry I helped build looks nothing like the one I started in. Instead of fighting the change, I became a bridge for it.

Today, I help companies integrate AI responsibly, rebuild their talent ecosystems, reorganize roles around human capability, create podcast experiences that elevate their brand, shift culture from expense-based thinking to investment-based thinking, and prepare for the workforce the future will require.

Everything we do today shapes what our children and grandchildren will inherit.

My grandfather used to say he was an old man with many worries, most of which never happened. Rock bottom teaches you that. Rock bottom strips away the lies and leaves only truth.

You have nothing to lose and everything to rebuild.

You rise because you must.

You rebuild because you are called to.

When no opportunity appears, you build the damn door.

If you want a partner who can help your company integrate AI without losing its humanity, you can find me through my show and speaking work because I bring the microphone to your people and the strategy to your leadership.

The future of work is human.

The future of work is rising.

About the Author

Jennifer Sheets is a CEO, author, podcast and radio host, and nationally recognized advisor on human capital strategy, workforce design, and the responsible integration of AI and emerging technologies. With more than 25 years of experience working alongside executive teams, founders, and high-performing organizations, she helps leaders strengthen their culture, align the right talent, and make decisions that produce both immediate impact and long-term return on investment.

As the founder and CEO of Jennifer Sheets CEO, she guides companies through complex people challenges—from scaling and restructuring to leadership development, retention, and modern workforce transformation. Her approach blends data-driven strategy with a deep understanding of human behavior, ensuring that organizations don't just hire talent, but accelerate the value that talent creates. She believes that people decisions are ultimately business decisions, and that when companies strategically invest in their workforce, everything from culture to profitability improves.

Jennifer is also the author of *Human Capital Lifeline*, where she explores how organizations can build resilient teams, navigate disruption, and integrate technology—including AI—without losing the human connection that drives innovation and trust. As the host of a podcast and radio show dedicated to leadership, culture, and organizational health, she brings meaningful conversations to audiences seeking clarity, confidence, and practical strategies in a rapidly changing world. She also offers **mobile podcasting services for corporate events, conferences, and on-site experiences**, allowing organizations to capture authentic stories and insights directly from their teams and leaders.

A sought-after **keynote speaker**, Jennifer inspires audiences with actionable strategies, transformative ideas, and a human-centered perspective on leadership. She is available to bring her insights, energy, and expertise to organizations seeking to motivate teams, spark innovation, and accelerate performance.

Her professional expertise is shaped not only by her corporate experience, but by her life experience as the mother of a pediatric cancer survivor. That journey instilled in her a profound understanding of resilience, advocacy, and the power of community—principles that influence her leadership style and her commitment to helping people thrive.

Jennifer partners with organizations across industries, delivering guidance that is strategic, direct, and actionable. Whether advising CEOs, supporting boards, or helping companies navigate change, she focuses on aligning people, purpose, and performance so organizations can achieve meaningful and measurable results.

Above all, Jennifer is passionate about ensuring that leaders maximize the investment they make in the talent surrounding them—because when people are empowered and aligned, companies grow stronger, cultures deepen, and outcomes improve across the board.

To learn more about her work or to explore partnership opportunities, visit **JenniferSheetsCEO.com**.

SCAN ME

CHAPTER SIX

The Three Core Challenges of CEO Leadership

By Tali Arviv, M.D.

As a CEO, success is rarely a straight line; it involves a continuous cycle of decisions, pivots, and personal growth. In my journey building and scaling businesses in medical aesthetics, I've identified three challenges that determine whether leadership translates into real impact: **Brand, Bodies, and Balance**. In this chapter, I'll illustrate what each challenge looks like in practice and how to strengthen each pillar without losing yourself in the process.

Consider these as the CEO's triad. The **Brand** represents your company's identity and its resonance in the world. **Bodies** refer to the driven, capable team members who bring that brand to life. **Balance** is the art of sustaining it all while maintaining your well-being and that of your loved ones. Drawing from my experiences, launching my first venture in 2014 and navigating expansions, sales, and reinventions, I'll explore each challenge in depth, sharing lessons learned, real-world examples, and strategies that can transform these potential pitfalls into strengths. Whether you're a startup founder navigating the early days or a seasoned executive managing a multinational corporation, these insights aim to empower you to lead with greater intention and effectiveness.

In the following pages, we'll delve into each element of the triad. I'll provide not just the what and why, but also the how: practical steps, pitfalls to avoid, and reflections from my career that have shaped my approach. By the end, you'll possess a roadmap to recognize these challenges and master them, ensuring your leadership creates a legacy of sustainable success.

The Brand: Building Trust Beyond the Logo

Brand is not merely your logo. It encompasses the trust people feel before they meet you and the consistency they experience afterward. Marketing generates attention, but brand fosters confidence, and confidence is essential for scaling.

When I launched my business in 2014, the marketing landscape was on the brink of transformation. The internet was dominated by SEO-optimized websites, Google Ads, and emerging Facebook campaigns. Instagram was just beginning to show potential, but much of our outreach still relied on traditional tactics: distributing flyers, business cards, and brochures at events or in waiting rooms. It was a blend of digital and physical realms, and as a new CEO, I dove in headfirst, eager to establish a foothold in the competitive world of medical aesthetics.

Back then, branding seemed straightforward: create a logo, choose a color palette, and maintain consistent messaging. For Arviv Medical Aesthetics, this meant a sleek, modern look that conveyed trust, a name that felt both professional and approachable, and simple marketing materials that reinforced our commitment to quality care. We focused on a few high-impact strategies: SEO to improve Google rankings, targeted Facebook ads to connect with local audiences, and Groupon to attract first-time visitors. This hands-on, grassroots marketing approach proved effective. When I opened the Miami location, one Groupon offer generated enough patients to convert into packages and cover rent as we built steady demand.

However, as my company expanded to three locations, I became immersed in the true art of brand building. Scaling required me to think beyond the basics. We weren't just growing geographically; we were enhancing our presence in consumers' minds. This journey involved continuous evolution—regularly updating our website to reflect the latest trends in user experience, refreshing our social media aesthetics to stay modern, and ensuring every touchpoint, from appointment reminders to in-office signage, felt cohesive. This wasn't about static identity; it was about adaptability. For instance, as Instagram gained traction, we shifted our focus to visual storytelling, sharing before-and-after photos (with patient consent), educational reels on procedures like Botox and fillers, and behind-the-scenes glimpses of our team. This evolution kept the brand fresh and relevant, attracting a younger demographic while retaining our core clients.

If you're in a regulated industry, build your platform with the same rigor you apply to your work. Consent, privacy, and ethical claims aren't optional; they're essential to the brand.

What truly propelled our success was the perception of scale and reliability that multiple locations provided. In consumers' eyes, a single-location business might seem boutique or niche, but expanding to three locations signaled stability and expertise. We established a stellar reputation at our flagship site in Tampa through exceptional service, word-of-mouth referrals, and consistent results. Once that trust was built, it transferred effortlessly to the new locations. Clients didn't question who was performing their treatments; they trusted the Arviv name. It didn't matter if a new injector was on staff—the brand's reliability drew them in. This taught me a crucial lesson: a strong brand acts as a trust multiplier, reducing the friction of growth and allowing you to scale without reinventing the wheel each time.

Yet, as any CEO knows, growth isn't always linear. Post-2020, demand surged as consumer behavior shifted with more remote work, increased self-focus, and heightened awareness of appearance on video. I expanded aggressively based on that spike, assuming the trend would continue. I increased the size of the Tampa office, opened a third location in Ocala, and launched a surgery center, all within one year. When the macro environment tightened in 2022, I felt the consequences of being overextended. The three locations, once symbols of success, became a strain. Previously, my marketing spend was under 5%, but suddenly I had to reconsider my marketing budget and enhance our social media presence. I found myself working harder, yet marketing costs rose without necessarily driving more business. They merely maintained the company's revenue flow and visibility.

To the outside world, I was seen as a successful entrepreneur, but I did not feel that way. I contemplated downsizing, but being naturally optimistic, I held on each month, hoping for a change in trajectory. Then, unexpectedly, I started receiving multiple emails and letters from private equity investors. Interest in a three-location med-spa prompted me to consider an exit. I felt humbled that investors were interested in my business. It was then that I truly recognized what I had built and its value. When I signed the final documents for the sale, I began to cry. I tried hard to hold it in, but it was an emotional moment. Initially, the exit felt like a defeat, but it freed me to refocus on myself. That's when I learned that sometimes the strongest move a CEO can make is not expanding but choosing an exit that allows for personal renewal and a new chapter. I decided to focus more on teaching, which led me to collaborate with my mom at the Medspa Institute.

I also redirected some attention to growing the surgery center, which had been somewhat neglected amid the expansion frenzy.

Then, a game-changing insight arrived. I hired a branding firm to help reposition the surgery center, and during our initial consultations, they articulated something no advisor had ever expressed: "Tali, *you* are the brand. You can take it anywhere, to any company." They emphasized that while corporate branding is important, personal branding is the ultimate portable asset. By stepping into the spotlight, sharing my expertise on labiaplasty, keloid treatments, and cosmetic dermatology through podcasts, social media live sessions, and industry panels, I could build direct trust with audiences. People don't just buy services; they buy into people. This shift from hiding behind the company name to owning my personal narrative was liberating.

Expanding on this, by personally branding myself, I've unlocked the ability to promote all my businesses simultaneously and strategically direct demand. For instance, after the sale, I leveraged my personal platform, my Instagram following, LinkedIn network, and speaking engagements to highlight not only the surgery center but also the aesthetics training and affiliate partnerships in aesthetics. If demand spikes for non-invasive treatments, I can direct traffic to Arviv Aesthetics and partner clinics; if surgical inquiries rise, I funnel them to my center. This flexibility is invaluable in volatile markets. Personal branding creates a central hub: me. From there, I can radiate influence across ventures, adapting to trends without being tied to one entity. It's like having a master key; my reputation opens doors, builds collaborations, and ensures sustainability.

To implement this, start by auditing your personal brand. What do you stand for? Share your story authentically, vulnerabilities included, to humanize your leadership. Use content marketing: blog about industry insights, create video series on leadership challenges, or host webinars. Measure success through engagement metrics and conversion rates. In my case, focusing on personal branding has helped expand my audience and open doors to new opportunities, such as training programs for injectors. CEOs, remember: your brand isn't just what you sell; it's who you are. Cultivate it wisely, and it becomes your most resilient asset, capable of weathering economic storms and pivoting with grace.

This evolution from corporate to personal branding has been transformative. It allows me to promote diverse businesses under one umbrella, my name, and direct business flows where they're most needed. Whether demand is high for aesthetics consultations or surgical procedures, I can channel it effectively, maximizing revenue and minimizing risk. It's a strategy every CEO should consider: build the company brand, but own your personal one. It's the bridge to endless possibilities.

Brand Audit (10 minutes)

1. What do customers assume about you before they meet you?
2. What do they feel after the first interaction: relief, trust, confusion, or pressure?
3. Where is the experience inconsistent (phone, front desk, consult, follow-up)?
4. If you opened a second location tomorrow, what would break first?
5. What proof builds trust fastest in your market (reviews, outcomes, referrals, content)?
6. What is one brand promise you can operationalize this week?

Closing Note: Watch for inconsistent experiences across touchpoints. Do this: operationalize one brand promise this week.

Bodies: Assembling the Right Team to Fuel Your Mission

No CEO succeeds in isolation. The second challenge, Bodies, refers to the essential human element: finding and retaining capable employees who align with your direction, mission, and brand. Over the years, I've encountered a spectrum of talent, but the standouts are those rare individuals with unyielding drive, genuine motivation, and a deep care for the business's success, as well as for you as the owner. These aren't just employees; they're partners in your vision, propelling the company forward with passion and precision.

Early on, as I scaled Arviv Medical Aesthetics, hiring was often reactive: a role opened, we posted it, sifted through resumes, and selected the most qualified candidate on paper. However, growth quickly taught me that credentials don't guarantee a good fit. I needed professionals who could embody the brand, protect the patient experience, and operate with ownership even when I wasn't in the room.

This shift forced me to stop hiring for tasks and start hiring for outcomes, behaviors, and alignment. Here's the simple framework I began using, which changed everything:

A Simple Hiring Framework (to avoid hiring on vibes)

1. Create a Role Scorecard (defining success):

    o   **Three outcomes** this role must produce (measurable results, not duties)

    o   **Three behaviors** this person must consistently demonstrate (how they work and treat people)

2. **Run a Values Interview (testing fit):** In interviews, I shifted from solely asking about experience to seeking proof of character, initiative,

resilience, ethical judgment, and customer care. While skills can be coached, character rarely changes.

3. **Set a 30/60/90 Plan (preventing slow starts from becoming failures):** Clear expectations eliminate confusion. When individuals understand what "good" looks like early, they stabilize faster, and you spend less time managing chaos.

Over time, I've been fortunate to work with truly unique team members: front desk staff who transformed routine check-ins into personalized consultations, injectors who ethically upsold add-ons, and managers who streamlined operations to enhance efficiency. These individuals didn't just "work" for the company; they helped carry it.

Another truth is that not every great hire shines immediately.

I've learned that employees can start slowly, struggling to adapt or grasp nuances, yet can become superstars with the right nurturing. For instance, one of my early hires in Tampa was a medical assistant fresh out of training. She initially found it challenging to navigate our fast-paced environment, making minor errors in scheduling and patient preparation. However, her attitude was impeccable: eager to learn, open to feedback, and genuinely invested in patient outcomes. Instead of letting her go, we invested in mentorship, pairing her with a senior team member and providing targeted training on our protocols. Within months, she became a key player, adding value by promoting our VIP program and driving revenue through upsells. This experience taught me the importance of patience in talent development: superstars aren't always immediate; sometimes, they are diamonds in the rough, polished through support and opportunity.

To uncover and cultivate talent, you must recruit with intention. Look beyond resumes and seek alignment in values, standards, and ownership. In interviews, ask for proof through stories that demonstrate initiative, resilience, coachability, and pressure management. Once they're onboard, clarify what 'great' looks like: set clear goals, provide autonomy with accountability, and publicly recognize achievements. I use brief shout-outs in team meetings to highlight actions that protect the brand, such as enhancing patient experiences, improving processes, or receiving positive reviews. Celebrating these actions encourages the team to replicate them.

Building relationships with staff is equally important, ensuring they consistently act in your best interest. This doesn't mean becoming best friends; it means fostering connections that promote loyalty and understanding. In my practices, I prioritize regular one-on-ones, not just for performance reviews but also to discuss career goals, personal challenges, and their vision for the business. This helps them understand my approach, emphasizing ethical sales, patient-first care, and continuous improvement. They intuitively grasp my expectations, delivering empathetic service, upholding rigorous standards, and innovating responsibly. When employees internalize your leadership style, they become extensions of you, making decisions aligned with the company's best interests even in your absence.

Moreover, the brand must be integral to every employee's character while at work; they must consistently deliver the standard. This means immersing them in the brand from day one. During onboarding, we don't just cover job duties; we explore the brand story: what Arviv stands for (trust, innovation, empowerment), how it differentiates us (personalized aesthetics with medical rigor), and why it matters (transforming lives through confidence). Role-playing exercises help them embody this, practicing consultations where they seamlessly integrate brand values. In daily operations, this translates to uniforms reflecting our sleek aesthetic, language that echoes our messaging (e.g., "empowering your natural beauty" instead of generic sales pitches), and behaviors prioritizing consistency. If an employee deviates, such as rushing a patient, they are gently coached back, not punished, to reinforce the brand as a living ethos.

Of course, there are pitfalls. Turnover can disrupt momentum, especially in high-demand fields like aesthetics where poaching is prevalent. Mismatched hires can dilute your brand, leading to inconsistent experiences that erode trust. To mitigate this, build a culture of mutual success: invest in ongoing training (e.g., lunch and learns for refreshers on sales, services, and products), promote from within to demonstrate growth paths, and lead by example, showcasing the drive and care you expect. I've also introduced incentives like performance bonuses tied to brand-aligned metrics, such as patient satisfaction scores, referral rates, and reviews. Even post-sale, I maintain connections with my team as the medical director, witnessing their care and dedication to the company and to me.

Retention becomes easier when people can envision a future with you. Tie incentives to behaviors that protect your brand, create visible growth paths, and invest in skill development that enhances their professional capabilities, not just their ability to work for you.

In essence, people are the lifeblood of your influence. The right team doesn't just execute tasks; they amplify your vision, transforming abstract goals into tangible results. By nurturing slow starters into superstars, forging inspiring relationships, and ensuring everyone embodies the brand, you cultivate a workforce that is resilient, aligned, and unstoppable. As CEOs, we must remember: our teams reflect our leadership. Invest in them wisely, and they'll carry your mission further than you could alone.

Closing Note: Be cautious of hiring based solely on credentials. Instead, hire for values and coach for skill.

Influence in Action™ for CEOs

Balance: The Art of Sustaining Success Without Sacrifice

Perhaps the most profound challenge for any CEO is balance, the delicate act of juggling professional ambitions with personal well-being and family life. In a role that's always "on," finding time to turn off can feel impossible. As a mother of three, the primary breadwinner, and a driven entrepreneur, this struggle is deeply personal and ongoing. It's not just about time management; it's about preserving your humanity amid the relentless pursuit of success.

Every day, if I arrive home at 6 or 7 p.m. instead of 5, a wave of guilt washes over me. I have support: a nanny, my mom, and my grandmother who reminds me regularly that children need us most when they're young. "When they're older, they won't need you, and you'll be looking for them," she says. "This is the time they want you. Be there." I believe her, yet reconciling that truth with the demands of running a business can be exhausting. I'm not only managing growth and decisions; I'm carrying the weight of family stability as the primary earner, which makes every call feel like high stakes.

After selling my practice, I still couldn't fully step back. I was promoting my personal brand through social media, networking, and consulting. However, I established a few non-negotiables to reclaim balance. Sundays are dedicated entirely to family time, regardless of other commitments. It's my reset; a time for play, cooking, lounging, and reconnecting with the people I'm working so hard for. Even during intense periods, I protect small moments for myself because self-care isn't selfish; it's essential for a leader's steadiness.

Family is undeniably important, but don't neglect your health; it's the foundation of everything else. Ignoring it leads to burnout, reduced focus, and a shorter fuse under pressure. For me, Pilates became my anchor. A colleague introduced me to it at a conference, and I was surprised by how quickly it strengthened my body and cleared my mind. Now, I schedule it a few days a week as an unmovable meeting. Not because I'm chasing fitness goals, but because it keeps me stable.

Nutrition is important because it protects performance. I've shifted from constant grab-and-go meals to simple, repeatable habits: prioritizing protein, opting for real meals over sugar spikes, and maintaining hydration throughout the day. The goal isn't a strict diet; it's leadership stamina. When I eat well and move consistently, I notice measurable differences: my energy remains steady, my decision-making stays clear late in the day, I'm more patient with my team, and I can be present for my family without feeling depleted. Small systems like meal prep, healthy office snacks, and a 'default lunch' make it manageable, even in busy seasons.

The path to balance isn't one-size-fits-all, especially in startups where resources are limited and every issue feels urgent. If you have the financial means, delegate to trusted lieutenants who can manage problems in your absence. Perhaps a COO for operations or a virtual assistant for administrative tasks. Set boundaries: define "off" hours (e.g., no emails after 8 p.m.), use tools like auto-responders to manage expectations, and communicate limits clearly to your team. I've implemented a "decision tree" system that ensures staff escalates only critical matters, allowing me to avoid micromanagement.

After 8 p.m., I'm offline unless it's urgent. If something is urgent, text me with: (1) what happened, (2) what you've already tried, (3) your recommended next step, and (4) what you need from me. If it can wait, document it, and we'll address it first thing tomorrow.

On Sundays, I'm unavailable unless it's a true emergency. If you're unsure, refer to the decision tree. Most issues can wait 12 hours without harming the business.

Yet challenges persist. In high-growth phases, such as launching a new location, boundaries blur and guilt intensifies, especially as a mom concerned about missing moments that won't come back. To counter this, I integrate my work calendar with my kids' schedules and block time for what matters: school activities, days off when they're out of school, and events like muffins with moms, plays, and the fall festival. It isn't perfect, but it's intentional, and intention is where balance begins.

For CEOs, balance is an ongoing optimization, not a destination. It requires self-awareness: regularly assess your energy levels, relationships, and health. Use apps for time tracking or journals for reflection. Remember, imbalance erodes influence. Exhausted leaders make poor decisions, and strained families sap motivation. By prioritizing family, engaging in activities like Pilates, and focusing on nutrition for sustained energy, you model holistic leadership. Your team observes it, your family feels it, and your business thrives because of it.

In facing these three challenges, Brand, Bodies, and Balance, I've transformed from a reactive entrepreneur to a purposeful influencer. Brand earns trust. Bodies deliver that trust. Balance sustains the leader who protects both. When one pillar weakens, the others eventually falter, but when all three are strong, your leadership becomes scalable. Master the triad, and you don't just run a company; you build an influence that lasts.

Closing Note: Be mindful of always-on leadership becoming your identity. To counter this, protect one non-negotiable boundary.

About the Author

Dr. Tali Arviv is a highly respected aesthetics provider, educator, and entrepreneur with more than 11 years of experience in aesthetic medicine. Known for her expertise, innovation, and patient-centered approach, she has built a dynamic presence in the industry and continues to shape the future of modern aesthetics.

Born in Israel and raised in the United States from the age of four, Dr. Arviv developed an early fascination with science and wellness. She completed her Bachelor of Science in Biology at the University of South Florida before earning her medical degree from Ross University School of Medicine. She went on to complete her Internal Medicine residency at Orlando Regional Medical Center, finishing in 2014—the same year she launched her first aesthetics practice.

Over the next decade, Dr. Arviv grew her practice into three successful locations across Tampa, Miami, and Ocala, becoming a recognized leader in aesthetic medicine. After ten years of expansion and development, she strategically exited ownership while continuing to serve as Medical Director for Arviv Medical Aesthetics.

Dr. Arviv is also the visionary behind 360 Surgery Center, a state-of-the-art, Quad A–accredited surgical facility where she performs minor surgical procedures and provides an advanced operating environment for fellow surgeons. Her commitment to excellence and safety is reflected in every aspect of the center.

Guided by her passion for teaching, Dr. Arviv founded the MedSpa Institute, a premier training platform dedicated to empowering medical providers through high-level, hands-on education. Her programs offer personalized, one-on-one instruction with live patients, as well as essential business resources such as patient implementation forms, consulting, marketing guidance, and operational strategies. Her mentorship helps practitioners build both clinical confidence and sustainable practice success.

Outside of medicine, Dr. Arviv is a mother of three who enjoys cooking, Pilates, and ballroom dancing—interests that reflect her creativity, discipline, and love for continual growth.

With her unique blend of clinical expertise, entrepreneurial vision, and devotion to education, Dr. Tali Arviv stands as a trusted mentor and influential leader in today's aesthetics industry.

www.medspa-institute.com

CHAPTER SEVEN

Leading Growth with Strategic Influence, Disciplined Capital Management, and Resilient Leadership

By Wayne Tupuola

Introduction: The Power of Leadership in High-Growth Industries

In high-growth sectors driven by innovation, successful leadership relies on more than breakthrough ideas. It hinges on your ability to influence stakeholders, manage capital judiciously, and foster organizational resilience to scale effectively while maintaining strategic control. In this chapter, I will translate lessons from capital markets and operational experience into a practical framework you can apply immediately: how to earn stakeholder trust, raise and structure capital wisely, negotiate terms that safeguard your future, and create a durable leadership playbook that withstands pressure.

Section 1: Influence as a Leadership FoundationHarnessing Influence to Drive Growth

Influence in high-growth companies goes beyond simple persuasion; it involves cultivating a compelling environment where stakeholders, investors, customers, employees, and partners trust your vision and believe in your leadership. This trust is essential for securing funding, forming strategic alliances, motivating your team, and navigating complex networks. To influence effectively, applying behavioral science principles, particularly those from Dr. Robert Cialdini's framework (with a few closely related principles combined for practical use), can provide a strategic advantage.

1. Authority: Demonstrating Expertise and Credibility People are naturally inclined to follow those perceived as knowledgeable and credible. Establishing authority involves showcasing your technical mastery, proven leadership, and industry experience through:

- Publishing technical white papers or thought leadership articles.
- Sharing success stories grounded in rigorous data.
- Receiving industry awards or endorsements that validate your expertise.

Impact on Growth: By positioning yourself and your company as authoritative, stakeholders are more likely to trust your judgment, support your initiatives financially, and champion your innovations. For example, when I highlighted our team's deep engineering expertise and environmental innovations in laser technology, investors viewed us as credible pioneers, simplifying funding negotiations. I've learned that authority isn't merely claimed; it's demonstrated. When we showcased our engineering capabilities, CleanTech differentiation, and the regulatory tailwinds supporting our solution, the conversation shifted from 'Is this real?' to 'How quickly can you scale it?' This transition reduced friction in due diligence and negotiations.

2. Social Proof: Validating Your Vision with Success Stories People often look to others' behaviors and opinions when uncertain. Highlighting successful case studies, customer testimonials, industry endorsements, or proven results creates social proof that your company's offerings are valuable and trustworthy.

Impact on Growth: Social proof reduces perceived risk for investors and customers, accelerates adoption, and builds momentum. By showcasing the environmental benefits and measurable cost savings of our laser cleaning systems, I convinced skeptics and attracted partners eager to align with validated innovations. One effective strategy was transforming outcomes into a repeatable narrative: a clear use case, measurable results, and a stakeholder quote. Consistently presenting these proof points, particularly around environmental impact and operational savings, shifted new conversations from skepticism to confidence, making partnerships easier to initiate and close.

3. Liking & Reciprocity: Building Genuine Relationships People prefer to work with those they like and trust. Authentic relationship-building involves transparency, mutual engagement, and delivering value without expecting immediate returns. Strategies include:

- Engaging genuinely with stakeholders and listening to their needs.
- Providing thoughtful support and resources.
- Publicly recognizing contributions.

Impact on Growth: Cultivating trust and goodwill fosters loyalty, encourages collaboration, and opens doors to strategic opportunities. In my experience, the strongest investor and partner relationships were established before urgent needs arose. By consistently sharing thoughtful updates, soliciting input early, and following through on commitments, negotiations became more collaborative, often resulting in faster alignment and more favorable terms due to pre-established trust.

4. Scarcity: Creating Urgency through Unique Value Scarcity highlights limited availability or unique opportunities to motivate swift action, which may stem from:

- Your company's exclusive technological patents.
- Limited market windows.
- Unique partnerships or first-mover advantages.

Impact on Growth: By emphasizing the rarity of your offerings or the time-sensitive nature of market opportunities, you stimulate stakeholders' desire to act promptly. For instance, positioning our laser tech as the sole solution capable of meeting emerging regulatory standards created compelling urgency for early adoption. We also learned to be precise with scarcity: focusing on timing rather than hype. When customers and partners recognized that evolving regulations and environmental standards were altering purchasing requirements, they viewed adoption as a strategic move to maintain compliance and competitiveness rather than a delayed option.

5. Consistency & Unity: Fostering Alignment Around Shared Purpose Consistency involves aligning your communication and actions with your core values and brand message. Unity refers to rallying your internal team and external stakeholders around a shared vision and purpose. Strategies include:

- Clearly articulating your mission and long-term goals.
- Demonstrating commitment through consistent messaging and actions.
- Creating organizational rituals and symbols that reinforce shared values.

Impact on Growth: When your internal team and external partners share a common purpose, they become more motivated and proactive. This unity enhances productivity and innovation while providing reassurance to investors and customers about your company's reliability and commitment to its mission. Internally, this alignment becomes evident when decisions reflect the mission rather than mere slogans. By linking priorities to a consistent message, CleanTech impact, engineering excellence, and disciplined execution, teams can make quicker decisions without second-guessing, and stakeholders perceive a company operating with clarity instead of confusion.

Influence Internally and Externally

Internally, cultivating a strong culture of shared purpose and transparent communication is essential. When your team understands and believes in the company's mission, it fosters alignment and a collective sense of ownership. Open dialogue about goals, challenges, and successes builds trust and inspires employees to contribute their best efforts.

Externally, confidence grounded in technical credibility and demonstrated social proof attracts partners, investors, and customers. Establishing authority through environmental benefits, industry validation, and proven results, such as during the development of our CleanTech laser cleaning system, secured critical funding and strategic alliances. These external signals enhance your reputation, extending your influence beyond internal teams and positioning your company as a credible leader in the industry.

In summary, harnessing influence requires a balanced approach: cultivating trust and credibility both within your organization and across the broader industry ecosystem. Internally, this involves nurturing shared purpose and open communication; externally, it's about showcasing your expertise and success stories to inspire confidence and attract essential stakeholders for sustained growth.

Influence isn't merely a soft skill; it's the gateway to resources. Once stakeholders trust your leadership, the next question becomes how to fund growth without jeopardizing your future. This is where disciplined capital management becomes crucial: it's not just about raising money, but about securing it on terms that preserve your ability to lead.

Section 2: Disciplined Capital Management—Ensuring Sustainable GrowthBalancing Funding with Control

Raising capital is vital for fueling growth, innovation, and market expansion. However, it carries inherent risks such as excessive dilution of ownership, loss of strategic control, and potential misallocation of resources. Navigating these challenges requires a disciplined, strategic approach that aligns your funding efforts with your long-term vision and operational integrity.

Key Principles for Effective Capital Management

1. Strategic Patience

- **Why it matters:** Rushing to close funding rounds before your technology, business model, or metrics achieve market validation can result in unfavorable terms, excessive dilution, or strategic rigidity.
- **How to implement:** Wait until your product demonstrates clear market traction, customer demand, and operational stability. This readiness provides leverage during negotiations, leading to better valuations, control rights, and favorable investor terms.
- **Lesson from experience:** Early in my career, accepting aggressive Seed round terms without sufficient validation led to rapid dilution, limiting our future flexibility. By postponing subsequent rounds until our product was market-ready, we negotiated better terms, protecting ownership and strategic independence.

2. Alignment of Investors and Long-Term Vision

- **Why It's Crucial:** Investors' goals must align with your company's strategic direction. Misaligned expectations can lead to conflicts, loss of control, or strategic pivots that undermine your vision.
- **How to Implement:** Conduct thorough due diligence on potential investors, prioritizing those with a history of supporting founders' visions and providing value beyond capital, such as strategic guidance or industry connections.
- **Practical Tip:** Seek investors whose investment horizons match your growth timeline and who are comfortable with your strategic approach, whether it involves aggressive scaling or steady growth.

3. Negotiation Discipline

- **Control Rights:** Safeguard core decision-making through veto rights, board seats, and protective provisions. Ensure you retain the ability to guide company strategy.
- **Anti-Dilution Clauses:** Protect early investors without overly restricting future funding flexibility. Capped or weighted-average anti-dilution provisions often provide a balanced approach.
- **Milestones and Triggers:** Clearly define metrics and performance benchmarks that determine funding releases or investor rights, reducing ambiguity and aligning incentives.
- **Implementation:** Prepare thoroughly before negotiations; understand your valuation range and identify non-negotiable rights (e.g., maintaining a majority voting stake and control over intellectual property).

4. Exploring Innovative Funding Options

- **Emerging Avenues:** Depending on your stage and market, options like SPACs (Special Purpose Acquisition Companies), blockchain financing, revenue-based financing, or hybrid debt-equity instruments can offer tailored solutions.

- **Advantages:** These options often provide more flexible terms, quicker access to capital, and strategic benefits suited for specific growth stages.
- **Caution:** Due diligence is essential to ensure compliance, transparency, and alignment with your strategic goals.

Lessons from Experience

- **Avoid Over-Aggressiveness:** Pursuing quick funding under unfavorable terms can lead to excessive dilution, fragility, and loss of control, limiting your company's future maneuverability.
- **Long-Term Perspective:** Patience and thorough due diligence during negotiations help secure more favorable valuations, control rights, and operational flexibility. For instance, delaying Series A until product validation provided leverage to negotiate better valuation and governance terms, establishing a stronger foundation for future growth.
- **Value of Timing:** Strategically waiting until your company is ready enables you to secure capital on your terms, rather than succumbing to immediate fundraising pressures.

Fostering a Funding Discipline Culture Embedding a culture of financial responsibility and strategic funding across your organization ensures capital is used effectively and purposefully:

- **Clear Principles:** Establish and communicate core guidelines, prioritizing ROI and avoiding unnecessary debt or equity dilution.
- **Rigorous Planning:** Develop detailed budgets, perform scenario analyses, and prepare contingency plans. Regularly update financial models to reflect changing realities.

- **Transparent Monitoring:** Use dashboards to track cash burn, liquidity, and progress against milestones. Conduct quarterly reviews for proactive course correction.

- **Data-Driven Decisions:** Leverage financial analytics, ROI calculations, and operational KPIs to inform funding requests and resource allocation.

- **Ownership & Accountability:** Assign clear financial responsibilities at all levels; each manager or department should be accountable for their budgets and performance metrics.

This disciplined environment ensures your organization deploys resources efficiently, aligns spending with strategic priorities, and maximizes growth potential while minimizing unnecessary risks.

Summary

Balancing funding with control requires strategic patience, alignment with a long-term vision, disciplined negotiations, and a culture of financial responsibility. Thoughtful fundraising approaches not only preserve your company's strategic integrity but also empower sustainable, scalable growth. Embedding these principles within your leadership philosophy ensures that each capital raise advances your mission without compromising control or operational agility, laying the groundwork for long-term success.

Section 3: Negotiating Funding Deals—Strategies for SuccessKey Deal Components

When engaging in funding negotiations, understanding and effectively managing these core components ensures the deal aligns with your long-term strategic goals while protecting your company's interests:

1. Valuation

- **Definition:** The process of determining your company's worth at a specific point in time.
- **Importance:** A fair valuation balances the capital raised with ownership dilution; overvaluation can lead to unrealistic expectations, while undervaluation may result in unnecessary dilution of founders and early investors.
- **How to Determine:** Leverage industry benchmarks, comparable companies, and financial projections. Incorporate growth forecasts, revenue potential, market size, and technological advantages to arrive at an informed valuation.
- **Best Practice:** Aim for a valuation that reflects your company's current traction and future potential, enabling you to raise sufficient capital without sacrificing excessive ownership.

2. Ownership & Control

- **Safeguards to Maintain Control:**
  - **Board Seats:** Secure reserved seats for founders or key executives to influence major decisions.
  - **Veto Rights:** Obtain veto rights over key actions such as fundraising, mergers, or asset sales.
  - **Protective Covenants:** Terms that prevent certain actions unless approved by founders or key stakeholders.
- **Why it Matters:** Retaining control ensures the company's strategic direction remains uncompromised by investor demands, enabling agility and preserving the original vision.
- **Negotiation Tip:** Balance control protections with investor needs to foster trust and long-term partnership.

3. Liquidation Preferences

- **Definition:** Terms specifying how proceeds from an exit (sale, IPO, liquidation) are distributed among shareholders.
- **Balanced Structures:**
  - **1x Non-Participating Preference:** Investors receive their original investment back before others but do not participate further.
  - **Participation Rights:** Investors receive their preference amount plus a share of remaining proceeds—a structure attractive for investors but potentially disproportionate for founders.
- **Your Goal:** Structure preferences to fairly reward early team members and founders, avoiding overly aggressive terms that could diminish their upside or complicate future exits.

4. Anti-Dilution Protection

- **Purpose:** Protect early investors from dilution if future funding rounds occur at a lower valuation ("down-rounds").
- **Types of Protection:**
  - **Full Ratchet:** Adjusts valuation automatically, potentially heavily diluting founders.
  - **Weighted-Average:** Limits dilution impact by considering the size and price of new investments; a more balanced approach.
- **Best Practice:** Negotiate capped or weighted-average anti-dilution clauses to maintain growth flexibility while protecting investors.

5. Governance Rights

- **Clarify Voting Rights:** Define decision-making processes, voting authority, and quorum requirements.
- **Board Composition:** Determine the number of directors, their appointing authority, and their scope of authority.

- **Protective Covenants:** Terms designed to safeguard investors' interests, such as approval rights for major transactions, issuance of new shares, or alterations to company bylaws.
- **Objective:** Ensure effective oversight while allowing founders to manage day-to-day operations. Proper governance structures enhance decision-making and align stakeholder interests.

Negotiation Strategy

To achieve a deal that benefits both your company and investors, adopt a deliberate, prepared, and flexible approach:

1. Thorough Preparation

- **Understand Your Valuation:** Assess your company's worth based on data and benchmarks.
- **Define Your Bottom Lines:** Identify non-negotiables, such as certain rights, valuation floors, or control terms.
- **Know Your Numbers:** Maintain clear financials, projections, and assumptions to support your valuation and deal structure.

2. Build Trust and Transparency

- Engage early and openly with potential investors.
- Communicate your company's vision, strategic plans, and challenges honestly.
- Cultivate credibility to foster collaborative negotiations rather than adversarial ones.

3. Prioritize Non-Negotiables

- Identify essential deal terms for maintaining strategic control or protecting your company's mission.
- Be flexible on valuation or other terms that do not compromise your core objectives.

4. Scenario Planning

- Prepare for various outcomes: best-case, worst-case, and most likely scenarios.
- Develop alternative proposals or trade-offs to ease negotiations.
- Anticipate investor concerns or objections and prepare responses aligned with your long-term goals.

5. Legal Documentation & Clarity

- Ensure all terms are clearly documented in definitive agreements.
- Engage experienced legal counsel with expertise in funding deals, term sheets, and investor rights.
- Clarity minimizes misunderstandings, disputes, and future renegotiations.

Summary

Effective negotiation aligns your company's strategic needs with your investors' interests through a comprehensive understanding of deal components. Meticulous preparation provides leverage: you'll know which terms safeguard your future, where you can be flexible, and what trade-offs are acceptable without losing control. By combining strong relationships with clear documentation and governance, you reduce surprises and build partnerships that can accelerate growth.

Section 4: Managing Investor Relations and Long-Term Partnerships

Securing capital is just the beginning. Maintaining investor trust and engagement is crucial as your company scales.

Best Practices

- **Transparency:** Regular updates on financials, milestones, and challenges foster trust.
- **Strategic Involvement:** Invite investors to contribute input on key decisions, leveraging their expertise and networks.
- **Clear Expectations:** Communicate growth plans and performance metrics.
- **Conflict Resolution:** Establish professional mechanisms for addressing disagreements, such as mediation, structured voting, or escalation pathways to uphold trust during challenges.
- **Celebrate Achievements:** Regularly share milestones like product launches, strategic agreements, or funding rounds. Acknowledging successes reinforces confidence and strengthens partnerships.
- **Align Interests:** Maintain ongoing dialogue to ensure investor expectations evolve with your company's growth, encouraging collaborative problem-solving instead of reactive conflicts.

Strong investor relations promote a partnership mindset, providing strategic resources, industry connections, and credibility that enhance your growth trajectory.

Section 5: Crafting Your Long-Term Funding and Growth Roadmap

A disciplined leader creates a clear and flexible funding strategy aligned with the company's vision.

Developing Your Funding Roadmap

- **Define Your Vision:** Identify target markets, key milestones, and product development goals, breaking them into short-, medium-, and long-term objectives.

- **Assess Capital Needs:** Utilize detailed financial modeling to project funding requirements at each stage—seed, Series A/B, expansion, and pre-IPO. Incorporate assumptions about growth, costs, and market opportunities. Scenario analysis helps understand best, worst, and most likely circumstances.

- **Identify Funding Sources & Timing:** Align funding sources with your development stages:
  - Seed & early stage: angel investors, crowdfunding
  - Growth: venture capital, strategic partners
  - Large-scale expansion: public markets, SPACs, alternative financing

Coordinate your funding timeline with product launches, key client acquisitions, or business milestones.

- **Maintain Flexibility:** Develop contingency plans to adapt to market shifts or internal changes. Diversify funding sources and review your roadmap regularly (quarterly or semi-annually).

- **Milestone-Linked Funding:** Connect funding rounds to operational goals such as technological validation, revenue targets, or regulatory approvals. This approach ensures disciplined progress and minimizes unnecessary capital raises.

- **Internal & External Alignment:** Communicate your roadmap across teams to ensure understanding of milestones, resource needs, and timing. Cultivate investor relationships early for rapid mobilization when necessary.

Section 6: Embodying Discipline and Flexibility as a LeaderFostering a Culture of Financial Discipline

- **Set Clear Financial Principles:** Establish core policies, only raise what's necessary, prioritize high-ROI initiatives, and avoid unnecessary debt or dilution.

- **Implement Rigorous Budgeting & Forecasting:** Use rolling forecasts and scenario planning, regularly reviewing actuals versus plans.

- **Ensure Transparency & Accountability:** Share financial metrics openly, cash runway, burn rate, operational costs, and hold managers accountable for budget adherence.

- **Leverage Data Analytics:** Utilize ROI, customer acquisition costs, and other KPIs to justify funding requests and optimize resource allocation.

Encouraging Innovation and Adaptability

- **Stay Abreast of New Funding Modalities:** Explore blockchain tokens, international crowdfunding, and strategic alliances tailored to your growth stage.

- **Pilot New Funding Models:** Test on a small scale, such as blockchain token offerings or hybrid debt-equity deals, before scaling.

- **Cultivate an Agile Decision Process:** Weekly reviews, real-time dashboards, and rapid feedback loops facilitate quick pivots.

- **Build Organizational Resilience:** Maintain financial buffers, reserve funds or credit lines, and develop contingency plans for supply chain disruptions or market shocks.

Resilient organizations blend discipline with flexibility, enabling swift responses to market dynamics while maintaining strategic focus.

Section 7: Developing Your Personal Leadership Playbook

To excel in complex funding environments, systematize your leadership approach:

- **Document Your Strategy:** Clarify your principles on funding, innovation, and resilience to serve as your decision compass.
- **Create Decision Trees:** Map scenarios like funding shortfalls, valuation fluctuations, or regulatory hurdles with predefined responses.
- **Build Your Network:** Foster relationships with prospective investors, advisors, legal counsel, and industry peers to ease the capital-raising process.
- **Regularly Review & Update:** Periodically revisit your playbook to incorporate lessons learned, evolving market conditions, or strategic shifts.

A well-crafted leadership playbook ensures disciplined, consistent decision-making aligned with your long-term vision.

Conclusion: Leading the Sustainable Growth Journey

Leading high-growth companies demands more than technological innovation; it requires mastery over influence, disciplined capital deployment, and organizational resilience. These core principles are interconnected:

- **Influence** secures stakeholder buy-in and strategic partnerships.
- **Discipline** ensures effective use of resources to meet milestones.
- **Resilience** enables robust adaptation amid uncertainties.

Drawing from my experience with Laser Photonics, I emphasize that sustainable success is rooted in purpose-driven leadership that fosters trust, makes informed decisions, and embraces adaptive change. Every critical choice, from team assembly to funding rounds, shapes your organization's future. Approach each decision with discipline, clarity, and flexibility to build a resilient organization capable of sustained growth and industry leadership.

Remember, leadership in high-growth industries requires a dynamic balance of vision with pragmatism, innovation with discipline, and agility with stability. By fostering influence, practicing disciplined financial management, and embedding resilience into your culture, you lay a foundation for long-term success that can withstand market fluctuations, technological disruptions, and competitive pressures.

Reflecting on my journey with Laser Photonics and the insights gained from steering a disruptive organization, I am convinced that technology alone does not guarantee victory. It is the disciplined application of leadership principles, trust-building, strategic resource allocation, and adaptable planning that transforms innovation into lasting impact.

As a leader, your role is to continuously refine these tools, proactively embrace change, and lead with purpose. Approach every decision, whether raising capital, managing teams, or navigating challenges, with intent and integrity.

The future belongs to those who lead thoughtfully and resiliently. By integrating influence, discipline, and flexibility into your leadership practice, you not only accelerate your company's growth but also establish a legacy of sustainable success and industry excellence.

Remember: Every decision you make today shapes your organization's tomorrow. Lead with purpose, stay disciplined, remain adaptable, and exceed your expectations.

About the Author

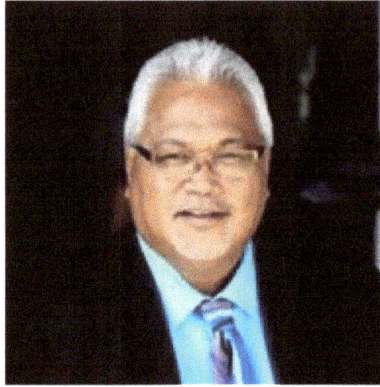

Wayne Tupuola is the CEO of Laser Photonics Corporation, a pioneering company in high-power fiber laser systems and laser-based manufacturing solutions. With over 15 years of executive leadership experience, Wayne has a proven track record of transforming industries through innovative technology and strategic vision. He is recognized for disrupting the traditional sandblasting industry by developing advanced laser cleaning equipment powered by proprietary CleanTech technology, revolutionizing surface preparation and cleaning across multiple sectors.

Wayne's career spans aerospace, semiconductors, and industrial manufacturing, giving him deep insight into capital-intensive operations, technological innovation, and market dynamics. His expertise includes navigating complex funding landscapes—such as private equity deals, venture rounds, and public market entries—combining technical knowledge with financial acumen. His leadership philosophy emphasizes transparency, disciplined negotiation, responsible innovation, and sustainable growth.

In addition to his corporate accomplishments, Wayne actively contributes to leadership development through his involvement with CEO Life, an organization dedicated to mentoring and coaching executive leaders. He holds BA in Communications from the University of Phoenix with over 25 years of engineering and executive management, blending a strong technical background with business expertise.

In this chapter, Wayne shares practical insights and lessons learned from his extensive experience, emphasizing how strategic capital management and disciplined leadership can turn innovative visions into market realities, driving long-term success and sustainability.

LASER PHOTONICS: https://lase.com

CHAPTER EIGHT

Business as a Passion: Following Your "North Star" Mission, Honoring Your Vision and Intent, Nurturing a Winning Culture

By Carol Ann Langford

Discovering the Mission – 'the North Star Why' of a Business

If you are reading this book, you are likely a business leader or entrepreneurial creator. Throughout your life, you may have felt an irresistible curiosity, drive, passion, or calling that motivated you to bring your vision, skills, and creativity to build your own business or contribute to an aligned team.

Many business owners recount knowing from an early age that they wanted to create something new, often requiring a less conventional path and reflecting a deeper sense of their true selves. These leaders describe purpose in various ways, but they all point to a common truth: mission comes from within.

For instance, in a 2016 interview with John Micklethwaite of Bloomberg News, **Jamie Dimon**, CEO of JPMorgan Chase, discusses his early, heart-centered quest:

- *"Since I was a kid, I've always wanted to help build a better society and a better company. I envisioned a healthy, vibrant company and society. We take care of our people and provide them with opportunities. I believe that what makes a great leader is heart, care, and curiosity. **Business is here to serve clients, shareholders, and communities. If we do this well, everyone benefits. We must do a good job for all of them.**"*
- In the words of **Whitney Wolfe Herd**, Founder of Bumble, during an interview on the Jamie Kern Lima Podcast: ***"The foundation of success is knowing your purpose in life, growing to reach your maximum potential, and sowing seeds that benefit others."***

If you resonate with this kind of inner discovery and recognize that there's something urging you toward a deeper, purpose-driven work life, then commend yourself for having *the courage* to heed that interior nudge and take action to follow your 'north star' intuition. Given the insights from these well-known leaders, regardless of where you are on your leadership journey, do you agree that trusting your inner truth is worth the risk of navigating the unknown in pursuit of your life's great adventure?

Here's what I hope you take away from this chapter: a straightforward method to identify your North Star Why, a clear Vision/Intention that translates purpose into direction, and a selection of cultural choices that transform values into daily behavior. You will see these elements woven through a true business story, followed by a practical set of skills you can apply to your leadership immediately. Purpose is beautiful; this chapter is about making it *usable.*

For more encouragement in accepting one's invitation to honor that sense of calling, a recent episode of the 'Diary of a CEO' podcast featured **Ray** Dalio, CEO of Bridgewater Associates. He identified one of his three favorite books as Joseph Campbell's classic, ***"The Hero With a Thousand***

Faces." Regarding the discovery of purpose, Campbell's compelling quotation invites us to:

"Follow your bliss {heart} and the universe will open doors for you where there were only walls."

Having listened to and collaborated with business leaders for 25 years as a Program Facilitator and Executive Coach within Fortune 500 companies, small and medium-sized businesses, startups, and NGOs, I have gained insights into what inspires them. It has been a joy to witness the positive transformational impact businesses have within their communities and to support the development of conscious leadership values, mechanisms, and skill sets.

An Early Example of a Mission-Driven Leader

On the topic of mission-driven leadership and the hero's journey, I'd like to share a compelling personal business story that illustrates the significance of having a mission, vision/intention, and culture designed for optimal business performance.

This true story features my brother, Rick, and my first husband, Mike, with whom I co-founded a business that still thrives today. I hope you find value and enjoyment in its telling.

As you read, I invite you to look for three threads: (1) Mission – the problem or promise that propelled us forward; (2) Vision/Intention – the specific decisions we made to scale that mission; and (3) Culture – the rituals and behaviors that made people feel seen, valued, and proud to belong.

To begin, Rick knew from an early age that he was meant to be a leader and businessman. His leadership journey started at just 7 years old when he became the President of his elementary school class, voted as 'Most Likely to Succeed.' He also sold Krispy Kreme donuts door to door in our modest suburb of North Springfield, Virginia, charging 20 cents for a package of six donuts. The neighborhood moms often gave him a quarter, encouraging him to keep the extra 5 cents as long as he returned with more donuts the following week. He learned early the profitable value of excellent customer service.

As Rick matured at age 10, he envisioned growth and expanded his services in the neighborhood to include lawn mowing, snow shoveling, and newspaper delivery on his bike in the mornings *and* evenings. At 15 years and 8 months, he obtained his Driver's License Learner's Permit and inherited a well-worn 1963 Chevy Impala, which he quickly leveraged to enhance his ambitions with a better job he could drive to. He found work at an automobile tire service shop, where he lied about his age, claiming to be 18, and started a 40-hour work week despite my school-teacher mom's objections.

Having lost our dad to alcoholism, there was a pressing need to supplement our mom's modest salary. I also worked after school in retail and babysitting until college, where I became Managing Editor of the student newspaper and then the first female President of the Student Government Association at James Madison University. Equipped with advanced secretarial skills from my high school business program, I secured a full-time Executive Assistant role at the U.S. Department of State during the summer, utilizing my speed stenography and typing skills along with a Top-Secret Security Clearance.

The **mission** was to keep our family afloat, while our vision was to secure high-level professional assignments with the best possible wages. Rick and I learned discipline and accountability early on, which helped maintain our family's stability. **Culturally,** we were aligned in performing our jobs to the best of our abilities to earn the highest wages and most advantageous benefits. The more we earned, the stronger our family bond became.

Rick's leadership charisma and technical skill in the automobile tire industry led to his rapid promotion at 18, making him the youngest manager of a local tire shop with the highest volume of business. He had a strong instinct for fostering a positive work culture, making the workplace feel like family for employees. His genuine love for his staff and customers, winning personality, advanced technical expertise, appreciation for premium retail aesthetics and cleanliness, and impeccable character all contributed to Rick becoming a leadership legend in the Northern Virginia automobile service sector.

Destiny arrived when my then-fiancée, Mike, moved to Northern Virginia to be closer to me. Mike was an exceptionally intelligent individual majoring in Political Philosophy at Williams College, gifted in winning debates and crafting innovative business models. Rick hired Mike at the tire store for the summer before our wedding, and before long, after numerous late-night dinner conversations about our shared interest in entrepreneurship, the three of us began planning to establish an automobile tire service business. We achieved that goal within a year, with Rick turning 19 on the day we opened and Mike and I at 22.

Our mission expanded as Rick and I transitioned into young adulthood. With the family system stabilized, we aimed to elevate the entire service industry by enhancing its practices.

A strong partnership developed among the three of us. Rick handled technical mastery and store organization, Mike negotiated favorable deals with suppliers and partners, while I focused on fostering a values-based leadership and management culture. Within just 18 months, we grew to nine flourishing shops and a thriving team.

A Takeaway Learning Here: Mission often emerges from necessity before it evolves into a brand statement. When your 'why' is genuine, your vision sharpens, and your culture becomes the foundation that enables people to endure and excel.

While we succeeded in transforming the tire service sector around Washington, D.C., a restless hunger for further growth simmered within each of us.

We shared an undeniable intuition and calling to fulfill a greater creative potential and expand our business and leadership endeavors.

After briefly wrestling with the question of whether we had reached our peak with the nine service locations, we recognized that we had more potential to develop.

The logical next step was to expand into the retail sales sector alongside our service offerings. We began exploring ideas for an additional business that would incorporate both retail sales and service in the automobile tire industry.

At that time, none of us had training or expertise in retail sales, but the deeper mission instinct and calling persisted; we pushed ourselves to embrace the challenge.

We learned that the retail tire market in the Northeast U.S. was heavily saturated with sellers, including some potentially influenced by organized crime. It quickly became clear that the tough competitive environment was not conducive to success. Expanding in our home turf of the Northeast Corridor seemed impossible. Nonetheless, we remained motivated and undaunted in our quest to grow. Here's what happened:

Given the crowded conditions in the Northeast, we sought out other viable locations for our next business venture. We conducted demographic studies of the fastest-growing cities in the United States, which at the time were Dallas, Texas, and San Jose, California. I insisted we choose San Jose as our ideal location. It was the perfect place to start anew, on the verge of explosive growth into what would become Silicon Valley. It felt right!

There was nearly infinite space to scale our passionate mission to build a great business where owners, employees, and customers would experience transformation, delighting everyone while elevating the retail automobile tire industry from a stereotypical junkyard mess to a premium brand known for cleanliness and an aesthetic of automotive beauty and coolness.

Rick's vision for the shops was captivating: pristine, clean, welcoming sales and service areas with elegantly painted floors and walls featuring framed photos and graphics of classic automobiles and Formula race cars. This inspiring design paralleled a culture that would be warm, welcoming, fascinating, and fun for customers and employees.

It was a bold vision. Did we wonder about failure? Yes. We considered the possibility that we might be overestimating our abilities. However, that thought did not deter us. We were young and confident that even if we failed, we could move on to something else. That 'inner knowing,' that nudge, that passion, and excitement for what felt like a destined adventure propelled us forward.

We sold the chain of nine service stores in the D.C. area and took leases on two premium warehouse spaces in Campbell and Santa Clara, California. With no real retail training or experience, and at the ages of 25 and 22, Rick, Mike, and I dove into the automobile retail tire sales and service business, flourishing almost immediately.

A Takeaway Learning Here: Vision and intention are not just moods; they are decisions that sometimes require courage. We didn't merely change locations; we moved toward an environment that could hold our futures, even if it meant leaving the beloved place that had been our home.

Our commitment to creating a great company culture led us to:

1. Pay the highest wages in the industry.
2. Provide the best benefits package.
3. Mentor employees in business ownership through profit sharing.
4. Provide exceptional customer service training and fostered a customer-obsessed culture where everyone who entered the shop felt like a cherished family member.
5. Host two large celebrations each year, one in summer and one in winter, inviting all employees and their spouses or significant others. During these events, generous bonuses, prizes, and special acknowledgments were awarded to everyone in the company.
6. Offer the best retail prices for customers.
7. Maintain beautiful store aesthetics and cleanliness.
8. Cultivate a word-of-mouth reputation as the best retail automobile tire sales and service company in the country.

One remarkable cultural practice that Rick upheld annually took place during the winter holidays. Even when the company grew to over 250 employees across 23 stores from north of San Francisco to south of Santa Cruz, Rick began preparing for this holiday ritual at the end of October. He wrote personal, customized holiday card notes to each employee, acknowledging their contributions to the company's success and elevated brand. He always found something distinctly positive to write and ensured he was informed about each employee's role in the business culture.

In addition to the personal notes, the cards included generous end-of-year bonus checks. Rick personally delivered each card at the beginning of December, making multiple trips to each store to present the cards in person to every employee.

During his visits, he took the time to shake hands, make eye contact, smile with appreciation, and engage in conversations about their personal lives, family members, and outside activities. He also inquired if the company could support any special causes or charities important to them.

YES - Rick made this effort for every single employee because he genuinely appreciated them and wanted them to feel that appreciation. He understood the importance of making people feel seen, recognized, valued, celebrated, and honored. This is why most employees remained with the company for many years.

Although Rick's motivation in expressing appreciation was sincere and not intended as a management tool, numerous studies indicate that when employees feel valued, they generally perform better. This observation aligns with decades of workplace engagement and motivation research showing that recognition, belonging, and psychological safety are strongly associated with performance retention and discretionary effort. When employees take pride in their company, they experience enhanced loyalty, a sense of belonging, and a stronger commitment to co-owning the company's success. Consequently, they invest more in the company's performance because they feel it belongs to them.

An important note about the impact of this caring company culture: the union attempted to organize the employees, but they voted it down in a resounding display of confidence and loyalty toward the company owners. This demonstrated their trust and enthusiasm for the company's mission, vision, and culture. It was a remarkable moment of solidarity that further strengthened these core values.

A Takeaway Learning Here: Culture is built through repeatable actions, not slogans. When people feel seen and protected, loyalty becomes genuine, and trust is earned in ways that no policy can manufacture.

After seven years of engagement in the launch and development of the company, I exited due to a new calling that led me down a different vocational path, while Rick and Mike continued to thrive in their mission, vision, culture, and leadership, growing the business to 23 successful locations in the extended San Francisco/San Jose Bay Area.

Another noteworthy story: Bridgestone/Firestone would send senior executives from Japan to tour all the U.S. businesses selling their products. During these visits, the executives consistently acknowledged Rick and Mike's company as *'not just the best in the United States, but the best in the whole world.'* Bridgestone/Firestone sought for years to acquire the business, but Rick and Mike remained steadfast, unwilling to cede ownership of a company that had become a happily cohesive professional family.

But in the year 2000, Bridgestone/Firestone made Rick and Mike an offer they could not refuse. After 25 years as partners, they felt it was time for a change and agreed to the buyout with a few conditions to maintain the culture cultivated over two decades. Rick and Mike continued as advisory managers for an extended period to safeguard that culture. The company still thrives today, 25 years after its acquisition, under the name Tires By Wheel Works. Building a steadfast business that lasts over 50 years is a remarkable achievement. I take pride in its ongoing legacy and must commend the endurance of its:

- Mission: to enhance and transform the retail automobile tire service industry.
- Vision: to create a sustainable, best-in-class, employee/customer-centric business model.
- Culture: honoring and elevating mutually beneficial relationships for optimum business processes and outcomes.

Skill Sets That Nurture Mission-Driven Leadership

The success of the story you've just read wasn't due to luck; it stemmed from specific *human* skill sets that made the Mission, Vision, and Culture repeatable. When leaders build relationships, communicate clearly, align intention with action, and resolve conflict, the North Star becomes a lived experience rather than just an idea. The skill sets listed below form the cultural fabric that sustains purpose when growth, stress, and change challenge your organization.

The following discussion provides a high-level overview of each skill set. A more in-depth examination can be found in my internationally best-selling book on Amazon, *The Speed of Passion: How Relationship-Based Leadership Drives Innovation* by Carol Ann Langford.

The Primary Skill Sets for Effective Leadership Are:

- Positive Relationship Building
- Executive Communication
- Brain/Heart Coherence in Setting Intention and Action
- Conflict Resolution and Transformation with Emotional, Social, and Cultural Intelligence

Positive Relationship Building

> *"Your job as a leader is not to lead as an individual but to foster an environment of co-elevation among your team. That's the key, because the team needs to become co-elevators of each other."*
> — **Keith Ferrazzi**

Steps for Nurturing Positive Relationships:

- Set a Vision/Intention to foster positive relationships with customers and team members.

- Assess stakeholders' connection to the meeting subject, their desired outcomes, any issues needing clarification, and the path to achieving those outcomes.

- Craft your narrative to meet others at their current level of understanding and guide them clearly to the desired level of acceptance and action.

- Pay attention to non-verbal cues and body language to enhance audience engagement and deepen connections.

- Remember the larger goal is to *nurture the relationships* that will bring about the envisioned outcome and transformation you have presented.

- Intend for a positive transformation with those attending the meeting.

Try This Tool: The Relationship Outcome Map (10 minutes before any meeting)

- Write the meeting topic at the top of the page.
- List the key stakeholders attending. Next to each name, note: **What do they care about most right now?**
- For each stakeholder, write one sentence: **For this person, success looks like ...**
- Determine your **one intended transformation** for the meeting: By the end, we will move from _____ to _____.

- Write your **one relationship action** to practice during the meeting (e.g., "reflect back concerns," "name shared goals," "invite input early").
- **Output:** A reusable one-page document for every high-stakes conversation.

"I know for sure that we each contribute to the whole of what it means to be a human on earth. The fullness of our humanity can be expressed only when we are true to ourselves. Your real job on earth is to become more of who you truly are. To live to the highest degree of what is pure, what is honest, what is natural, what feels like the real you. Anything less is a fake life. To be authentic is the highest form of praise. You're fulfilling your mission and purpose on earth when you honor the real you."

— Oprah

Executive Communication – Using the Content Navigator

- Be clear about your listeners' knowledge and understanding of the subject.
- Let your preparation and expertise instill confidence, allowing you to maintain authenticity and honor your presence.
- What does it mean to be a steward of oneself?
- Know the subject thoroughly.
- Create an introduction using your Perspective Statement, a Recommendation for the Audience, and your Vision for the best Outcome.
- Let the Body of the Message provide necessary data and explanations with Focus Points and Supporting Points.
- Conclude with a powerful closing Perspective, Actionable Recommendation, and Vision for the Best Outcome.

Try this Tool: The 60-Second Executive Opening (Content Navigator Notes)

Before your next meeting, write your opening as follows:

Perspective (1 sentence): "Here's what I'm seeing…"

Recommendation (1 sentence): "Here's what I recommend we do…"

Vision/Outcome (1 sentence): "If we do this, success will look like…" Then limit your body to 3 focus points (no more), each with one supporting proof (data point, example, or customer impact).

Output: A 60-second opening and a 3-point body outline you can deliver without rambling.

- Review the Body Language Coaching Sheet.
- Frame Body Language within the context of 'values-based leadership,' ensuring balanced posture conveys Respect, Movement fosters Inclusion, Gestures signify Authenticity, Facial Expression communicates Good Will, Pausing ensures Coherence, Eye Contact builds Trust, and Voice promotes Transparency.
- Bring your authentic self and personality to every interaction.

Neuroscience and Brain/Heart Coherence in Setting Intention and Action

Neuroscience is the next frontier in management.
Optimizing leaders' brains will soon be a critical source of competitive advantage in the business world.
— Stephen Bochner, MD

> *Extraordinary things happen*
> *when we harness the power of the brain and heart.*
> — **Dr. James Doty, Neurosurgeon**

Steps in Setting Intention:

- Get quiet in mind and body; connect with an open heart.
- Imagine your goal or aspiration; envision it fulfilled.
- Find gratitude in advance of the fulfilled vision.
- Take necessary actions to achieve your goal.

Try This Tool: The Coherence-to-Action Micro-Ritual (5 minutes)

- **Get Quiet** (60 seconds): Take a slow breath in, then a slow breath out, and soften your shoulders.
- **Name one intention:** "In this meeting/conversation, I intend to..."
- **Choose one emotion to lead with** (gratitude, courage, steadiness, goodwill).
- **Pick one aligned action:** "The action I will take today is..."
- **Close with a checkpoint:** "Afterward, I will reflect on whether my action matched my intention."

Output: One sentence of intention plus one specific action you can hold yourself accountable to.

Conflict Resolution and Transformation with Emotional, Social, and Cultural Intelligence

We believe that conflict is inevitable, but violence is not. Conflict arises naturally from human diversity. When we approach conflict adversarially, it breeds polarization and violence. Conversely, collaboration can catalyze positive change. Our vision is a world where cooperation is the norm—where differences stimulate social progress instead of violence.

- Search for Common Ground (the largest peace-building organization in the world, serving 35 countries and nominated for the Nobel Peace Prize in 2018).

Steps for Transforming Conflict:

- Cleanse your perception by seeing the 'other' as clearly as possible, without the cloud of projection that often accompanies difficult relationships. Acknowledge your role in the conflict. Where are you accountable for the pain?
- Don't take anything personally.
- Choose to tolerate differences; truly lay down your emotional and relational weapons.
- Build on what you have in common. Actively seek knowledge of shared interests that may lead to wonderfully creative outcomes.
- Use the aikido politics mechanism to 'protect your opponent' while transforming the hostility directed at you.
- Deliberately pursue an authentic path to forgiveness. Most people are doing their best. Try to see the situation from others' perspectives and assume innocence on their part.
- Use inquiry to learn more about the situation, aiming to increase understanding and dispel any misconceptions.
- Use advocacy to honor the other person or team by assuming positive intent and finding the generosity to align with them.
- Remember that, fundamentally, we're all on the same side in the grand scheme. Identify the common goals everyone shares and express appreciation for their participation in the aspiration.
- Choose radical compassion in your outlook. Pay it forward with generosity of spirit. Be deliberate in your expressions of goodwill toward everyone.

- Celebrate all the steps above, knowing that if you practice them, your karmic bank account will double and triple in value in the short term. In other words, choose professional love; it's your best bet and greatest investment with the highest return. You'll also feel happier, and your brain will function better.

Try This Tool: A Common Ground Script (for difficult conversations)

Use this 5-line script the next time tension rises:

- **"Here's what I think matters most to you..."** (reflect their value)
- **"Here's what matters most to me..."** (state your value)
- **"What we both want is..."** (name common ground)
- **"Where I may be accountable is..."** (own your part)
- **"A fair next step would be..."** (one concrete action + timeline)

Output: One shared goal + one next step you can document in writing.

In closing this chapter's reflection on business as a passion, following your 'North Star' Mission, it's important to acknowledge the moment we're in. Across the United States and around the world, familiar cultural norms are being disrupted by unprecedented and unpredictable change. The rapid adoption of AI, robotics, and innovation, alongside major social, scientific, and environmental shifts, can leave people feeling ungrounded and uncertain. My intention here is not to debate politics; it is to recognize the reality many communities are facing: the ground is shifting, and people need stability.

Historically, people often look to large institutions to respond to distress, whether it stems from conflict, disaster, economic disruption, or rapid cultural change. Regardless of where solutions originate, there is a practical truth we can act on immediately: businesses influence daily life.

Workplaces shape how people experience dignity, stability, belonging, and hope. When the world feels chaotic and uncertain, mission-driven leaders have an opportunity to provide a steady presence, one decision, one policy, one act of care at a time.

With these conditions in mind, I'd like to call on business owners and leaders across our nation to step in with positive assistance wherever possible and aligned with elevated values. Listen for the prompt from your deeper self: your intuition, your better angels, your common sense. Choose a constructive way to be an awake, alert, sane, responsible, caring presence through which unnecessary conflict and suffering can be alleviated. For some leaders, this may mean protecting dignity at work through fair pay and humane schedules; for others, it may involve training and opportunities for those displaced by change; for some, it may entail ethical technology choices, community partnerships, or simply fostering a culture of respect and calm. However you express it, let your business become a compassionate and stabilizing presence, guided by your North Star Mission and demonstrated through your culture.

As Mike Sharrow, CEO of C12 Business Forums, has noted, when we prioritize families, communities, and future generations, we must elevate the role of business as a spiritual and social engine. Business can shape culture, forge futures, and strengthen the foundation of communities.

Let us nurture and protect the communities around us for the greater good, positive growth, and transformative change. We can achieve this by aligning ourselves with a North Star Mission, defining a clear Vision and Intention, and fostering a Culture where dignity, responsibility, and compassion are practiced consistently, especially during challenging times.

Try this Tool: Your "North Star Worksheet (Quick Draft) Template

Mission (Why): We exist to _____ so that _____.

Vision/Intention (Where we're going + how we choose to lead): We are building toward _____. We will do it by _____.

Culture (What we practice): We will reinforce our values through these three repeatable behaviors/rituals: 1) _____ 2) _____ 3) _____."

Onward!!

The above information is from Carol Ann Langford's *The Speed of Passion: How Relationship-Based Leadership Drives Innovation*.

For inquiries about hiring Carol Ann Langford for Executive Coaching, Facilitation, Training Classes, or Keynote Speaking, please contact her at Carol@LangfordLeadership.com.

About the Author

Carol carries an inspired passion for developing people as an executive coach, facilitator, and keynote speaker. She has served in the corporate organizational development space for 20+ years. Carol is known in her coaching for holding highest standards among her clients in bringing intentional vision and ownership to their leadership and delivering exceptional results through their teams.

As a Coach and Facilitator, Carol's work has occurred in Fortune 500 companies to startups within industries including Consulting, Banking, Health Care, Retail, Real Estate, Insurance, Big Tech, Pharmaceutical, Advertising, Publishing. The list of clients she has worked with includes Korn Ferry, Deloitte, KPMG, Capital One, PayPal, Amazon, Apple, State Farm, Fidelity, Flextronics, Moody's Investor Service, Pfizer, Monsanto, Ferguson Partners, Stax Private Equity, Tregaron Private Equity, Cogleus, PowersHealth, ImageThink, SeatGeek, State Farm, Chromatic among others.

As the Founder of Langford LLC, Carol specializes in Strategic Leadership, Executive Presence, Influencing and Persuasion, Consultative Dialogue, Strategic Negotiation, Conflict Transformation, and Neuroplasticity for Enhanced Human Performance. She carries a Professional Coaching Certification (PCC) with the International Coach Federation, a Master of Fine Arts degree from New York University Tisch School of the Arts, certificates in 'Conflict Transformation' from Baltimore Mediation and Search for Common Ground. Within the field of neuroscience and brain-based approaches to leadership development, Carol is a Certified Consultant with Dr. Joe Dispenza's NeuroChangeSolutions group. She is also certified for Emotional, Social, Cultural Intelligence via programs including Conversational Intelligence with the CreatingWe Institute, Shirzad Chamine's Positive Intelligence, Mike Dooley's Infinite Possibilities.

As an author, Carol has recently written an Amazon International Best-Selling business leadership book entitled '*The Speed of Passion: How Relationship-Based Leadership Drives Innovation.*' Part textbook, story-telling, motivation, and a view for the neuroscience-based future of leadership, readers are delighted in Carol's practical approach to developing leaders. Her book was also acknowledged by the well-known *Book Excellence Review* as the best leadership book for 2023.

Additionally, Carol and *The Speed of Passion* have been featured in numerous articles in notable periodicals such as USA Today, International Business Times, Benzinga, Business Insider, and online tv and radio interviews including Jack Canfield's 'Talking About Success,' Kate Delaney's 'America Tonight,' Close up TV's Doug Llewelyn and Jim Masters shows, Spark TV's Logan Crawford among others. She was a featured author in 2023 and 2024 at the London Book Fair and the University of San Diego Festival of Books.

Carol's writing has also been featured in the *Tony Robbins endorsed* '*Cracking the Rich Code*' in which she discusses the relevance of 'leading with empathy in a VUCA world.' Carol continues to receive requests for interviews from a wide variety of print, digital, radio and tv media journalists.

Further, Carol was recently inducted into the prestigious Marquis 'Who's Who of America.'

Prior to her corporate training and coaching vocation, Carol served for seven years as Associate Professor at City University of New York where she taught a global population in Humanities. Classes included English Composition, Principles in Dialogic Communication, Public Speaking, Storytelling.

Carol enjoys a parallel career path in the non-profit sector where she served as Director of Disbursements for a modest family foundation and fundraising advocate for premium brand ngo's. This work has taken Carol on service trips to Sierra Leone, West Africa for conflict transformation (Search for Common Ground); Nicaragua for micro-lending to small business owners (Opportunity International Board of Governors 2006-16); the Amazon Rainforest for environmental sustainability (The Pachamama Alliance). She serves on the Leadership Council of Convergence Center in Washington, D.C. and is a former Board member of the Collegiate Corporation and Deacon of Marble Collegiate Church.

After college, Carol taught high school English, co-founded a successful retail company, acted and wrote for the professional theatre. She values lifelong learning and continues to take a wide variety of classes for professional and personal development. Carol resides in Park Slope, Brooklyn and loves film, theatre, museums, and all the fulfillment which attends living in the diverse environment of New York City.

CHAPTER NINE

Sparks and Bonfires

By Douglas S. King, CFP®

When I first sat down to outline this chapter, I wondered, "What *could I possibly offer fellow CEOs that they haven't already heard?*" As I pondered this, the answer became clear: almost everything I know that works was learned from others.

For decades, I've maintained a simple journal. Whenever I read a passage that resonated, heard a memorable line, or attended a workshop that shifted my perspective, I recorded it. Those pages became a portable advisory board. When real-world problems arose, missed targets, a reluctant team member, a key client at risk, I didn't attempt to invent something new. Instead, I pulled out my journal, reviewed the years of collected wisdom, recalled what mattered most, and put those insights to work.

Over the years, I have never confused originality with impact. I've taken sparks from many minds and, through disciplined execution, built bonfires from them. Influence in action rarely stems from the cleverest thought; it's about curating the right ideas, aligning the right people, and transforming insights into repeatable outcomes.

Whenever possible, I'll attribute lines and frameworks to the leaders who taught me. In the spirit of leadership as a relay, I believe many would acknowledge that they originally heard these concepts from someone who cared enough to pass them on.

By the end of this chapter, you'll have a straightforward field guide to use immediately: a concise set of repeatable leadership behaviors, and the rhythm to practice them, so your influence translates into trust, performance, and lasting sales.

A Short Origin Story

I grew up in Richmond, Virginia, during the early 1960s. My mother was a teenager raising three kids, my older sister, my half-brother, and me. For most of my childhood, my stepfather struggled with alcohol and often failed to show love. He taught me, sometimes harshly, who I did not want to become. I didn't meet my biological father until I was twenty-eight.

Money was tight. My mother initially did not work outside the home, and my stepfather barely earned enough to support a family of five. I learned early that if I wanted decent clothes or a path to college, I had to earn it. While my own home lacked the father figure I needed, I was fortunate to observe the fathers of my four best friends model engaged fatherhood; they quietly taught me the kind of dad I aspired to be.

I've been an entrepreneur for as long as I can remember. I started my first "company" at six, selling candy to other kids in elementary school. I learned early that I preferred merit pay to hourly wages, and without truly understanding it, I began building small sales teams to achieve goals I couldn't reach alone. At age eight, I started a lawn care business, purchased the equipment, and hired neighborhood boys to help manage the 52 homes we serviced. I began newspaper routes in grade school and college, hiring others to deliver the papers while keeping the profits for myself. In college, I launched a franchise selling trips to Fort Lauderdale over spring break and ski resorts during winter break. By my senior year, I had 12 friends and fraternity brothers selling trips, filling over 20 buses for their destinations. That inclination toward ownership, and enrolling others, has remained with me.

Professionally, I began as a Financial Advisor right out of college. Over thirty-one years, I led other advisors at national firms, assisted companies in expanding, and in 2020 launched a family-run suite of national financial services firms dedicated to helping business owners and families with nearly every financial aspect they encounter. I also served on more than 30 volunteer boards, chairing 10 of them, including the CFP Board of Standards.

Today, I have the rare privilege of working alongside my wife, our four adult children, and a talented team of professionals. My sons are CFP® professionals, IRS Enrolled Agents, and Certified Financial Fiduciaries. They serve as licensed advisors and principals across our brokerage, advisory, insurance, and accounting firms. Building a multi-disciplinary, values-aligned team both at home and at work has been one of the greatest joys of my life.

Those early lessons shaped my current beliefs: what drives results isn't what you claim to value; it's the choices you make under pressure and the routines you maintain when nobody's watching.

What Mattered Most (Looking Back)

If you had asked me thirty years ago to list the milestones that shaped me, I would have started with the language we were all taught: Values. Vision. Strategy. Mission. Goals. Scorecards. Those concepts matter greatly. However, age and experience add a layer of discernment. The factors that truly drove results were rarely the posters on the wall. They were the choices we made under pressure, the habits we established after a win, the relationships we mended when trust waned, and the operating cadences we maintained when nobody was watching.

Whether by plan, luck, or divine intervention, I made some good choices. In these pages, I'll share those that changed our trajectory. You'll recognize many of them. That's the point. Influence isn't a trick; it's the disciplined practice of ideas you already believe, applied at the right moment, with the right people, in the right way.

That's why the principles outlined here are written as behaviors rather than ideals. Values don't scale until they transform into habits, and habits don't stick until they are placed on a cadence. The Bees discussed below are simply the behaviors I've observed that compound trust, first at home, then across teams, and finally in the marketplace.

Opening

I used to believe a CEO's job was to have the best ideas in the room. After forty years, I know better. The best ideas rarely originate with us; they pass through us. My advantage has never been originality; it's been curation and execution. I've spent a lifetime collecting insights from people wiser than me and turning those insights into bonfires, translating values into habits, aligning people to purpose, and establishing the cadences that fulfill promises. That's **influence in** action: measurable trust, fewer escalations, faster decisions, more renewals, and more yeses without discounting.

This chapter serves as a field guide to the principles that have made a significant impact in my companies and my life. You won't find slogans here; instead, you'll discover choices, how to prioritize *family* while building enduring enterprises, how to define *legacy* through the people you shape rather than the titles you hold, and how to lead through a set of simple, repeatable behaviors I call **"Follow the** Bees." Each Bee is accompanied by a brief story or practice that you can apply in your business.

Lead with authority, and you may achieve compliance. Lead with influence, grounded in character, consistency, and clarity, and you earn commitment. Commitment shortens sales cycles, improves margins, deepens loyalty, and ensures that wins stay won. The ideas that follow aren't new. Used together, they illustrate how I've helped transform sparks into sustainable, compounding results.

Family First

If 'family first' sounds soft in a tough business world, consider this: it's a leadership strategy. When you protect what matters most, you lead with clarity, and your people deliver their best because they trust your priorities.

I met my wife, Katy, in third grade. We went to prom together, married young, and built a life centered around family. As my career accelerated, I made time for her with scheduled date nights, dance lessons, dinners with friends, and trips around the world.

We raised four children together and prioritized being present in their lives. We encouraged them to participate in sports while coaching their soccer, baseball, football, and kickball teams. We led them in scouting as the scout leaders for our three Eagle Scout sons and our Silver and Venture Scout daughter. We also instilled a love for the outdoors through countless ski, scuba, hiking, biking, hunting, and fishing trips together.

All four children chose to work with us in the family business, not out of obligation, but because they recognized meaningful work and a team that enjoyed doing it together.

"Family" is not defined solely by blood. It includes your employees and executives, your clients and their families, your business partners, and your in-laws along with their extended relatives. It encompasses anyone you care about and who holds significance in your life.

"Family first" is not just a slogan. It embodies presence when it matters, modeling character under pressure, and celebrating small victories loudly. It also entails upholding standards, honesty, humility, and courage, applied with grace. The result is influence that resonates: your children, teammates, and clients will reflect your consistent actions.

CEO Actions:

- Block non-negotiable family time on the same calendar used for investors and clients.
- Treat significant moments (performances, games, graduations) like board meetings: planned, prepared, and never missed.
- Allow your team to witness you protecting these priorities; they'll feel encouraged to do the same, and will return with more energy to their work.

Build Your Legacy

When you're gone, titles fade. What endures is how people felt around you and who they became because of you. My children observed me fail, reset, and try again. They saw me coach with high standards and a bigger heart. They witnessed me pursue ambitious dreams, and then invited me into theirs. That is legacy: the transfer of courage, character, and craft from one generation to the next.

Legacy is also forged in partnerships. Be honest and fair with those who choose to build alongside you. Keep your word, even when it's costly. Teach through your decisions. Remember that influence compounds: every dinner, vacation, and call taken in a crisis deposit into a relationship that will outlast any quarterly report.

CEO Actions:

- Define three behaviors you want your family and company to inherit from you. Practice them daily and highlight them publicly when you see others embody the same.
- Build friendships intentionally, both inside and outside your industry. Leaders who invest in community make better decisions and navigate tougher seasons.

Follow the Bees

Bees That Set the Emotional Climate

This first set of bees will help you shape the atmosphere before you even discuss strategy. If you manage the emotional climate well, the rest of leadership becomes easier.

Be Happy

Smile often; it's contagious. A smile lowers defenses, opens conversations, and sets a tone people want to follow. When a CEO enjoys their work and can laugh at their own quirks, it gives everyone else permission to show up fully, try boldly, and recover quickly. Happy leaders notice what's working and celebrate small wins; that optimism doesn't ignore reality; it fuels resilience.

Happy Points

Every morning, you wake up with **10 Happy Points**. Little frictions, such as annoying alarms, stubbed toes, hot coffee, and traffic, try to withdraw from this account. You decide whether to let each moment take a point. You can also **earn** more points: a warm hello at reception, a specific compliment to a teammate, or a quick note of gratitude to a client. Don't allow yourself or a stranger on the highway to spend your balance. Aim to arrive at the office with all ten points and go to bed with even more. Happiness is a habit, and presence makes it possible. By guarding your emotional balance, you make clearer decisions, and your team feels steadier around you.

CEO Action:

Make Two Deposits: Before noon each day, create two Happy Point deposits: one public micro-celebration and one private, specific thank-you.

Be Positive

A positive attitude shapes outcomes and manifests in your habits, choices, discipline, and conversations, elevating everyone's energy and well-being.

Positivity isn't pretending; it's disciplined optimism. It acknowledges reality *and* possibility in the same breath, then chooses to build on what's working. A positive CEO sets the emotional baseline for the room: calm, constructive, and forward-leaning. This climate enhances performance because it boosts belief.

CEO Action:

Start with Progress: Open every 1:1 and staff meeting with one concrete improvement since the last meeting, 60 seconds each, no speeches.

Be Patient

Patience protects potential, both yours and others'. Goals deserve urgency, while people deserve time. Growth is uneven; some weeks may seem stagnant, then compounding effects appear all at once. Be patient with those learning and doing the work, but be impatient with waste that hinders progress. Patience prevents over-correction after a setback and allows standards to take root.

CEO Action:

24-hour rule: For one meaningful people decision, pause 24 hours to gather one more perspective before acting.

Be Encouraging

Encouragement fuels growth. It isn't flattery; it's specific, earned confidence that recognizes what someone is doing right and inspires them to reach the next level. Encouraging leaders catch people doing the right things, praise in public, coach in private, and create a safe environment to try, learn, and try again. This belief compounds: teams take smarter risks, recover faster, and remain engaged longer.

In my twenties, I met Chuck, a shoeshine man with a world-class smile and a slow lobby. I invited him to set up inside our office during wholesaler lunches. It worked. He added days, bought a second stand, hired help, and expanded to four locations. The last time I saw him, he thanked me for believing in him before he believed in himself.

That's the power of encouragement: it transfers belief long enough for people to build their own.

CEO Action:

Hand the mic: Spotlight a rising leader by allowing them to present a win or lead a segment; you introduce, and they own the moment.

Bees That Build Trust and Psychological Safety

This next set of Bees encourages honesty and engagement during challenging times. Trust accelerates communication; when people feel safe, they share the truth more quickly.

Be Loving

Love is demonstrated through action. Lead with care, patience, and generosity. People don't care how much you know until they see how much you care.

I strive to show love by being present at crucial moments, coaching with high standards and a bigger heart, and treating partners and clients fairly, even at a cost. In business, love is not soft; it is disciplined care: establishing clear expectations, providing honest feedback, prioritizing suitability, and making decisions that benefit everyone involved, clients, partners, and ourselves. When people feel valued, they give their best and remain committed.

"What makes us human is not our mind but our heart, not our ability to think but our ability to love."
— **Henri J.M. Nouwen**

CEO Action:

Make time visible: Schedule two 15-minute blocks this week, one to walk the floor and thank people by name, and another to call a client to express specific appreciation (no agenda).

Be Respectful

Respect is influence in everyday interactions. It manifests in small habits that accumulate: learning and pronouncing names correctly, starting and ending meetings on time, making eye contact, and listening fully before responding.

Respect allows for disagreement without diminishing others. It preserves dignity in public, provides constructive feedback in private, and treats vendors and junior staff with the same courtesy as board members.

When people feel respected, they engage, voice their opinions, and perform their best work.

CEO Action:

Names & Time: Learn (and use) the names of three colleagues you rarely address by name, and conclude your next team meeting five minutes early to honor everyone's time.

Be Forgiving

When a CEO forgives quickly and openly, it reduces fear, retains top talent after honest mistakes, and refocuses everyone on learning and improvement. Start by forgiving yourself: laugh at your own missteps, acknowledge them publicly, and demonstrate how you resolved the root cause. With others, differentiate good-faith mistakes (made while pursuing the right goals) from carelessness or misalignment. Forgive promptly and codify the lessons; coach firmly when patterns persist. A forgiving culture is not weak; it is proactive. It shifts from blame to improvement, from shame to standards, and from fear to initiative.

CEO Action:

Model It: Share a recent mistake of your own with the staff, offer a brief apology, and explain the fix and its due date.

Be Honest

Always be honest, especially with yourself. Speak the truth even when it is costly.

Always do what is right simply because it is right—**"stay on the side of the angels."** In my world, we are fiduciaries; the law requires us to act in clients' best interests. However, integrity transcends compliance. The standard must be personal long before it becomes legal.

CEO Action:

Be impeccable with your word. Imagine a perfect, smooth sheet of paper. Now crumple it into a tight ball, open it, and attempt to smooth it out. You can't; the creases remain. Trust operates in a similar manner: once it's damaged, you may repair the relationship, but the wrinkles never fully disappear. Protect your words and promises accordingly.

Be Transparent

To build trust, you must be open with your employees and managers. Establish clear channels of communication. Listen to your employees' ideas. Lead with questions rather than answers. Create a forum for input and creative ideas, then take action and report back so people can see their contributions reflected in the outcome.

Companies that earn the hearts and minds of their employees will serve their customers better because individuals who feel heard tend to give their best.

CEO Action:

Lead with questions: In your next review, ask: *What do you see? What do you recommend? What support do you need?* Only then provide your answer.

Be Empathetic

Empathy is disciplined curiosity. As Stephen Covey teaches in *The 7 Habits of Highly Effective People*, you should 'seek first to understand, then to be understood.' When you perceive the world from another person's perspective, including their pressures, hopes, and constraints, you make better decisions and earn lasting trust. Empathy doesn't lower standards; it makes them resonate. It transforms feedback from a threat into a form of assistance.

CEO Action:

Three before me: Ask three clarifying questions before proposing a solution: *What matters most? What's blocking you? What have you tried?*

Be Kind

Kindness isn't weakness; it's strategic. It maintains dignity during disagreements, facilitates difficult feedback, and keeps doors open with customers and partners. Extend the same courtesy to vendors and junior staff that you offer to your board.

CEO Action:

Two kindnesses: Perform one visible act of kindness at work (public thanks) and one invisible act of kindness (quiet help) today.

Be Genuine and Present in the Moment

Genuine leadership involves quiet alignment, where your words, motives, and behaviors match. It means dropping the performance, withholding quick judgments, and prioritizing service over showmanship. It also has practical aspects: putting your phone away in the presence of others, refraining from comparing your path to anyone else's, and being honest about what you know and don't know. When leaders are authentic, teams feel at ease and bring their best selves to the work.

Be fully present when others speak. The more someone discusses themselves, the more they like and trust you, as they feel seen and heard.

CEO Action:

Be phone-free: For one day, keep your phone out of sight during every conversation. Look people in the eye; notice the difference.

Be Humble

Humility isn't thinking less of yourself; it's thinking of yourself less. It involves being able to laugh at your quirks, ask for help, and give credit before taking it. Humility makes you more coachable and encourages others to share the unvarnished truth with you. It also accelerates growth; when you acknowledge gaps, you can work to close them.

CEO Action:

Credit Transfer: Publicly recognize three individuals for recent successes, and specify the behaviors you wish to see repeated.

Bees That Drive Execution and Reliability

This group of Bees transforms good intentions into follow-through and measurable outcomes. Execution is where credibility becomes tangible.

Be Intentional

Value each day. Choose your mindset and act purposefully. Great outcomes rarely occur by chance; they arise from clear priorities pursued intentionally. Intentional leaders determine what matters, align their time and energy accordingly, and kindly but firmly say no to distractions.

As John C. Maxwell states, "You'll never change your life until you change something you do daily. The secret of your success is found in your daily routine." Purpose leads to practice, which leads to proof.

CEO Action:

Daily Top 3: Each morning, identify the three outcomes that most advance your mission. Prioritize time for these first and protect those time blocks.

Be Committed

Commitment means completion. It involves following through on your promises. Victory goes to those who finish, not just those who begin. The final 10% is where trust is established: closing loops, keeping promises, and completing tasks without excuses.

Challenges are not interruptions; they are opportunities for growth. When a CEO consistently finishes tasks, teams adopt the habit, customers experience reliability, and results accumulate.

CEO Action:

Promises Ledger: Publish a simple "promises made / promises kept" note each Friday until it becomes second nature.

Be Responsible

Take ownership of your mistakes. When results fall short, look in the mirror first; avoid blaming employees, bad luck, or external factors. While some elements will always be beyond your control, effective leadership means owning what you can and moving the company forward regardless.

Be accountable for your life, decisions, actions, and results. Responsibility links effort to outcomes, transforms regret into actionable plans, and rebuilds trust faster than any speech.

Responsibility involves not only owning mistakes but also teaching stewardship, so those you lead do not repeat costly lessons.

Educate your children and employees about the **time value of money** to encourage early saving and investing. Share this story about Bob and Bill:

- Bob invests $200 monthly from age 21 to 29 (9 years), earning 8% annually, then stops at 30 and lets his investment grow.

- Bill waits until age 30 to start investing $200 monthly until he is 65 (35 years), earning 8% annually throughout.
- Which one has more money at age 65?
- Bob contributed $21,600, and his investment grew to $465,530.02 by age 65.
- Bill contributed $84,000 but started later, and his investment grew to $458,776.50 by age 65.

Bottom line: The earlier you start saving and investing, the more your money compounds, requiring less cash to achieve the same (or better) outcome.

Be Proactive

Take responsibility for what you can control (Covey). Make the first move, surface risks early, and ask for what you need. Proactive leaders don't wait for perfect information; they start, learn, and adjust.

CEO Action:

Pre-read the decision: Send a 3-line note before the next big meeting: *What we're deciding, options considered, recommended next step.*

Be Persistent

Consistency beats intensity. Keep the main thing the main thing until it's done. Obstacles are expected; persistence transforms them into landmarks along the way. Stay focused on your goals and refuse to quit when challenges arise.

"Success requires continuous effort
and the refusal to give up when faced with obstacles."
— Napoleon Hill

CEO Action:

Eight-week rule: Choose one priority and maintain the same metric, owner, and cadence for eight straight weeks. No new goals until this one sticks (similar to Gino Wickman's Traction theory).

Be a Planner

John J. Beckley said, *"Most people don't plan to fail; they fail to plan."* He likely drew that from Benjamin Franklin, who stated, *"Those who fail to plan, plan to fail."* Stephen Covey's Habit #2 adds the operating system: Begin with the end in mind.

As a CFP® professional, planning is in my DNA. I believe it's the key to success. With families and small businesses, we map a path from Point A (where you are) to Point B (where you want to go), keeping you safe and on track by anticipating changes and adjusting as needed. We run our companies the same way.

Create your succession plan today. Most owners never articulate their endgame because they are busy with daily fires. Decide now: Why are you building this? Will you pass it to children or partners, or sell it someday? When you start with the end in mind, every future decision improves and brings you closer to that outcome.

Cash is king. Great companies fail not for lack of sales, but for lack of cash discipline. If cash management isn't your strength, partner with someone who can build a Cash Management Plan to prevent running out.

CEO Action:

One-page Endgame: Write your exit on a single page: *Keep/Pass/Sell*, target timing, success criteria, and share it with your leadership team.

Bees That Expand Capacity and Leadership Reach

This final set of Bees enhances your influence, decision quality, and long-term legacy. This is how you build a leadership legacy that endures.

Be Confident

Believe in yourself and in your team. **Act boldly** and take the right risks.

Refuse to live in fear of failure. As an entrepreneur, you already know that failure is part of the process. Own the lessons, reset, and move forward.

CEO Action:

Borrowed confidence: Identify one area where your team needs your steadiness. Clearly and calmly state the decision, the reason behind it, and the first next step.

Be Influential

As John Maxwell reminds us in *The 21 Irrefutable Laws of Leadership*, leadership isn't about your position; it's about your influence.

Build a culture based on values you genuinely uphold. Hire the right people, place them in suitable roles (Jim Collins, *Built to Last*), and delegate tasks to capable individuals. Coach them beforehand, not afterward. Influence grows when others can make decisions independently.

CEO Action:

Pass the pen: Allow a rising leader to make a decision you would typically own; coach them on the criteria in advance, then support their choice.

Be Courageous

Believe in yourself and the team you've assembled. Take calculated risks, set Big Hairy Audacious Goals (BHAGs), and pursue them. Expect more from yourself than from others, and lead by example.

Courage, as Brené Brown describes in *Dare to Lead*, involves ignoring naysayers, doing what's unpopular, admitting your mistakes, bouncing back from failure, stepping out before feeling ready, speaking with confidence, recognizing your worth, and embodying the leader you wish you had.

Establish character guardrails by making decisions in advance about who you will be under pressure.

Don't take things personally; others' actions reflect their own issues. Protect your Happy Points.

Play to win rather than to avoid losing. Have the courage to let poor fits go when they cannot or will not meet your standards.

CEO Action:

Right seat move: Today, either delegate one role you still hold or begin the hiring and development plan to fill it.

Be Transformative

View the world differently; start with small steps and invite others on your journey. Your actions may spark change. Don't settle for average.

"I want to make a difference with people who make a difference, doing something that makes a difference."
— **John Maxwell**

CEO Action:

Encode the fix: After solving a recurring problem, institutionalize it with a new checklist, contract clause, or CRM field to ensure it remains resolved.

Be Smart

Never stop learning. Stay updated on markets and technology; embrace AI while maintaining critical thinking. Read books or listen to audiobooks during your commute.

Remember Covey's lesson in Habit 7: Sharpen the Saw.

CEO Action:

Read to apply: Select one idea from your current book and implement it within seven days; report the results to your team.

Be Generous

Compensate your employees well, then compensate yourself afterward. Research and offer slightly above-market wages once your company is profitable.

Create incentive programs for key executives, or for all employees if possible, based on overall company profitability (e.g., a profit-sharing plan with year-end bonuses tied to performance).

Provide a strong company benefits plan, including a company-sponsored 401(k) with matches and ROTH contribution options.

Give back to your community and involve your employees in projects that are meaningful to you.

CEO Action:

Pick a charity and organize a company-sponsored event for all employees to participate in. Provide them with time off work to engage in these activities. Ideas could include volunteering for a day with Habitat for Humanity, adopting a family at Christmas and delivering toys to the children, or preparing Thanksgiving food baskets for those in need.

Be Quiet

I'm still working on this one. Listen more than you speak and aim to be the last to share your thoughts.

I first recognized the power of this while watching the old **E.F. Hutton** commercials: when the room quieted, people listened. Earn that kind of attention by speaking less and adding value when you do.

CEO Action:

Last word, best word: In your next discussion, summarize others' points first; share your view only after every voice is heard.

Be Introspective

Make time for yourself. My motto has always been, "Work hard; play harder." I've tried to instill that in my kids, employees, and clients because real work/life balance fuels motivation, energy, and creative thinking. When I'm not working, I intentionally step away so I can return sharper.

Ask questions about everything. If you disagree with someone, invite them to help you understand their perspective (religion, politics, values, whatever matters to them). Listen, and you might learn something new.

In high school, a friend once said, "Doug, you're always asking questions!" I hadn't realized it until that moment, but it was true. I questioned everything, not to prove I was right, but to learn: how things work, why people hold certain beliefs, and what I might be missing. Years later, people ask, "How do you know so much about so many things?" The answer is simple: I kept asking, never assumed I already knew, and never assumed I was hearing the whole story.

CEO Action:

Three questions first: In your next disagreement, ask three sincere questions before sharing your view: *What matters most? What am I missing? What would good look like for you?*

Be Exceptional

"You attract who you are; to attract better people, become the kind of person you want to attract." (Maxwell) Excellence draws excellence.

Be the type of person you want to meet. Be a living example of excellence to your team.

"If your actions inspire others to dream more,
do more, and become more, you are a leader."
— John Quincy Adams

Some people say I've had a successful career and life. Whether or not that's true, I can honestly say I've always given it my best. If there's one lesson I hope you take from this chapter, it's this: success isn't a single spark; it's a bonfire built on repeatable choices.

Here's a simple way to put this into motion: choose three Bees that could most transform your leadership climate right now. Practice them for seven days. Schedule the CEO Actions on your calendar. Inform your leadership team which three you're focusing on, and ask them to hold you accountable. At the end of the week, share any changes in morale, decisions, execution, or trust, and keep the ones that made a difference.

If you do this week after week, you won't just collect sparks; you'll build something lasting. Ultimately, I hope you measure success the way the best leaders do.

Ralph Waldo Emerson captured it well in his poem:

Definition of Success

- *To laugh often and much.*
- *To win the respect of intelligent people and the affection of children.*
- *To earn the appreciation of honest critics and endure the betrayal of false friends.*
- *To appreciate beauty.*
- *To find the best in others.*
- *To leave the world a bit better, whether by*
- *a healthy child,*
- *a garden patch,*
- *or a redeeming social condition.*
- *To know even one life has breathed easier because you have lived.*
- *This is to have succeeded.*

I wish you the very best in your business and life, and I hope you turn the right sparks into bonfires.

Douglas S. King

About the Author

Douglas S. King, CFP®
President & CEO, Oakwood Capital Partners, LLC

Doug King is a CERTIFIED FINANCIAL PLANNER™ with over 40 years of experience helping families, business owners, and fellow advisors navigate complex financial decisions with clarity and care. He is the founder and CEO of **Oakwood Capital Partners, LLC** (dba "Oakwood Capital"), the management company for a coordinated suite of five Oakwood Capital-branded financial services firms.

Under Doug's leadership, **Oakwood Capital** operates with a dual focus:

1. **Back Office Support for Financial Firms**

Oakwood Capital, Inc. (a Registered Investment Adviser), Oakwood Capital Securities, Inc. (an independent broker-dealer), Oakwood Capital Insurance Solutions, LLC (an Insurance Marketing Organization), and Oakwood Capital Accounting & Tax Advisors, LLC together form a unified back-office platform that supports independent advisors and boutique financial services firms.

These entities provide financial professionals who wish to maintain their own company brand with fully integrated services across investment operations, asset management platforms, compliance, technology platforms, insurance solutions, marketing, and fractional CFO services. This centralized model enables them to focus on serving their clients—while benefiting from Oakwood's scale, infrastructure, and fiduciary-centered expertise.

2. Direct Client Services

Oakwood Capital Advisors, LLC is a wealth management firm that caters to financial advisors seeking to utilize the Oakwood Capital brand while leveraging the back-office services of other Oakwood Capital firms. All advisors follow a consistent and disciplined asset management philosophy, with a strong emphasis on financial planning, business advisory services, and long-term client relationships.

Before founding the Oakwood Capital firms, Doug held senior roles at Merrill Lynch, Bank of America, and Cetera Financial Group, and has led other RIA and insurance marketing organizations. He earned dual bachelor's degrees in finance and management from Virginia Tech and an MBA from the University of Minnesota's Carlson School of Management. Doug obtained his CFP® designation in 1989 and holds multiple securities registrations.

Doug has served extensively in industry and community leadership, including five years on the CFP Board of Standards, where he served as Board Chair in 2021, and is currently a member of the board of the Northern Star Council of the Boy Scouts of America. He has also held leadership roles with the Minneapolis Regional Chamber of Commerce, the American Heart Association, Rotary International, and numerous other nonprofit organizations. Additionally, he has coached numerous youth sports teams and served as a Scoutmaster to his three Eagle Scout sons.

Doug and his wife, Katy—his childhood sweetheart and partner for nearly 40 years—have four adult children, all of whom are actively involved and are owners in the Oakwood companies. He enjoys spending time outdoors with family, especially fishing, hunting, hiking, kayaking, snowboarding, and riding his Harley.

CHAPTER TEN

Taxes, Taxes, and Taxes!
Learn to Pay as Little as Laws Allow!

By Chris Craig

The Tax Cut and Jobs Act (TCJA) has introduced the most significant tax changes since 1986. However, most of these changes are scheduled to expire at midnight on December 31, 2025. This situation can be likened to the Cinderella problem, where tax cuts replace the concern of her carriage turning into a pumpkin at midnight!

In this chapter, I will guide you on how to structure your company effectively, consider the differences between W-2 income and pass-through income, identify loss limitations that may obstruct your strategy, and plan ahead to retain more of your earnings legally. You'll receive a simple checklist to use with your tax advisor to identify missed opportunities and avoid costly mistakes.

Business Owner Takeaway: Changes in tax policy are crucial because they affect your deductions, the timing of income, the way losses offset other income, and whether your entity structure benefits you or hinders you. My focus is not on politics but on helping you retain more of your earnings legally by planning early, structuring wisely, and avoiding pitfalls that often trap high-performing business owners.

Why the TCJA Timeline Matters

Here's the concise version of the TCJA narrative that you need as a business owner. We will then immediately address actionable steps because knowledge alone will not reduce your tax bill.

The TCJA introduced major tax reforms, with many provisions scheduled to sunset, creating a built-in deadline. This is why 2025 is a critical year: businesses and households face a future where the rules could change unpredictably and swiftly.

As lawmakers debated extensions and funding methods, projections and estimates varied widely based on different assumptions and baselines. While this variability is common in tax policy, it poses a challenge for business owners: you cannot formulate a solid tax strategy based on last-minute guesses.

The key takeaway from this political landscape is that uncertainty presents a tax risk. Waiting until the final year limits your options. By planning early, considering entity structure, compensation strategy, deduction timing, and loss planning, you create choices for yourself. Now, let's discuss the actions that truly matter.

Different baselines = different numbers.

Quick Note: Why Estimates Vary

Some estimates assume temporary provisions will expire ("current law"), while others assume Congress will extend them ("current policy"). The same policy idea can yield different outcomes based on starting points.

Regardless of the trending bill name or the headline-making package, the pattern remains unchanged: tax rules shift, deadlines emerge, and those who plan early reap the rewards. Now, let's move from the noise in Washington to what you can control within your business.

What Business Owners Should Do Now (Not Later)

Now, let's get practical. The aim is not to memorize the tax code but to create a structure that allows you to keep more of your earnings legally, year after year. We'll start with the rules that can trip up business owners who believe they are doing everything correctly.

With the context established, here's what should matter most to you as a business owner: taxes directly reduce your company's capacity to reinvest, hire, and expand. The sooner you properly structure your entity and income streams, the more options you will have. More upfront options lead to fewer last-minute decisions and mistakes.

"Anyone may so arrange his affairs that his taxes shall be as low as possible; he is not bound to choose that pattern which will best pay the Treasury; there is not even a patriotic duty to increase one's taxes." ***Helvering v. Gregory***, 69 F.2d 809, 810-11 (2d Cir. 1934).

"Courts have repeatedly stated that there is nothing wrong with arranging one's affairs to minimize taxes. Everyone does it, rich or poor, and it is right because no one has a public duty to pay more than the law requires: taxes are enforced exactions, not voluntary contributions. To demand more in the name of morals is mere cant." ***Commissioner v. Newman***, 159 F2d 848 (1947).

This chapter focuses on legal tax planning, not tax evasion. The objective is to understand the rules, structure your finances correctly, document them accurately, and remain compliant. Use this chapter as an educational tool, then partner with a qualified CPA/EA to implement the right strategy for your situation.

Section 461(l) presents challenges for W-2 income and S-Corp distributions. This law, in effect since 2020, restricts taxpayers from offsetting active income with business losses.

Section 461(l): The "Excess Business Loss" Trap Business Owners Don't See Coming

Let's discuss a rule that catches successful business owners off guard because it seems inapplicable to them. Section 461(I) limits how much "business loss" can offset other income in a given year. In simple terms, even if your business reports a significant loss, you may not be able to use the entire loss to eliminate your income for that year.

What it does (in plain English)

If your business incurs a loss exceeding a certain threshold, the IRS may classify the "extra" portion as an excess business loss. This excess typically cannot offset other income in the same year as many owners expect. Instead, it usually gets carried forward and treated similarly to a net operating loss (NOL) in subsequent years, meaning you may benefit later but not when you need it most.

Who gets surprised by it

This rule often affects individuals doing well because the higher your income, the more noticeable it becomes when a loss cannot fully offset it. Common profiles caught off guard include:

- Owners with W-2 income (or a high-earning spouse) alongside a business reporting "paper losses."

- Pass-through owners (S-corps/partnerships) with significant deductions or one-time write-offs.
- Real estate and operating businesses showing a large loss in a single year due to depreciation or accelerated deductions.
- Anyone assuming, "If my K-1 indicates a loss, I can apply it against all income."

A simple example (round numbers)

Imagine your household has $400,000 in W-2 income. Your business reports a $500,000 loss this year due to equipment purchases, expansion, or substantial deductions. Many owners think: "Great, my business loss offsets my income."

However, under Section 461(I), you might only be able to use part of that loss to offset this year's income, while the remainder becomes a carryforward. Consequently, you still owe taxes this year, often unexpectedly, because the "loss" did not function as you assumed.

What to do about it (legally)

Here are practical planning steps to discuss with your CPA (this is not legal advice, just smart questions):

- **Plan deductions and timing:** If you can control when deductions occur, you might spread them across years instead of creating a "giant loss year" subject to limitations.
- **Coordinate income strategy:** If you're choosing between W-2 salary, distributions, bonuses, or other compensation timing, model how the mix impacts the ability to use losses.
- **Model multiple scenarios before year-end:** Don't wait until tax filing season. Conduct an estimated tax projection in Q3/Q4 to avoid surprises in April.

5 questions to ask your CPA this week

- "Based on our projected numbers, will Section 461(I) limit how much of our business loss we can use this year?"
- "If we are limited, how does the unused portion carry forward, and when can we realistically expect to benefit?"
- "What year-end actions most significantly affect this rule (timing deductions, timing income, depreciation elections, entity decisions)?"
- "How should we adjust estimated taxes to avoid unexpected liabilities?"
- "What documentation do we need to support our positions if the IRS questions us later?"

Bottom line: Business owners do not lose money merely because tax rates change; they lose when they assume deductions automatically lead to lower taxes in the current year. Section 461(I) is one of those rules that makes planning and timing essential.

About the Author

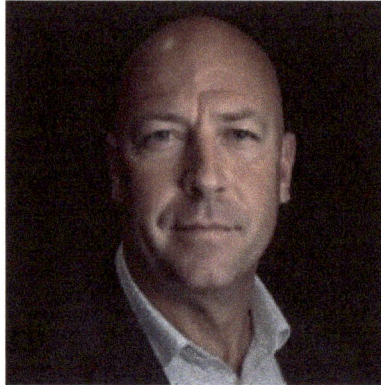

Christopher Craig is an Enrolled Agent and Certified Tax Planner licensed to practice before the Internal Revenue Service. He earned a master's of business administration from the University of Phoenix, a Master of Laws from Thomas Jefferson School of Law in Taxation and Business Bankruptcy. Chris has been engaged for the Law Offices of Steven L. Yarmy from 2009-2024, as an Insolvency and Restructuring Advisor and is affiliated with Hunter Parker LLC, law firms. Chris has successfully developed financial plans of reorganization in over 200-chapter 11 business reorganization cases and currently consults with multiple law firms in multiple states. He was a past member of The Association of Insolvency and Restructuring Advisors, www.aira.org, and the Turnaround Management Association.

Chris is also a United States Marine who has served in the Marine Corps honorably from 1993-2000. Chris has been involved in many technical startup companies and spent the majority of his career in distressed real estate and turn around management. Chris is married to Cristina, and has two children 11 years old and 5 years old.

You may schedule a discovery call with Chris at www.thetaxfirm.us to go over your specific tax issues or planning questions.

CHAPTER ELEVEN
People, People, People

By Alex Hernandez

In real estate, they say the three most important words are: *Location, location, location.*

In business, I believe the three most important words are: *People, people, people.*

You can have the best strategy, sharpest branding, and the most appealing location equipped with the latest technology, but if you don't have the right people in the right roles, supported in the right way, you're just decorating a sinking ship.

At the end of the day, everything comes down to people:

- The individuals you hire.
- The way you treat them.
- The tools you provide.
- The culture you foster.

I've seen organizations spend months obsessing over dashboards and KPIs while neglecting the very people responsible for those numbers. KPIs matter. Performance matters, but those metrics are merely the scoreboard.

The members of your team are the players, and if you don't invest in them, you can't be surprised when you don't make the playoffs, let alone the Super Bowl.

Give People the Tools and then Hold Them Accountable

When you talk to a manager about underperformers and ask, "Did Stark or Athena receive everything they need to succeed?" you're often met with silence... or excuses.

That's when you need to slow down and get specific:

- Did they receive proper training?
- Did someone show them what "good" looks like?
- Did they get coaching, not just criticism?
- Did they have the tools, time, and support to improve?

When you press on those specifics, too often the response is, "I've been too busy," or "I didn't have time."

Simply put, that's unacceptable.

As a leader, this is your number one controllable area. You *must* make the time. Shame on us if we don't.

You cannot fairly take someone through a performance process, write-ups and corrective action, if they never truly received the tools and support they needed in the first place. If they weren't properly equipped, then you haven't done your job as a leader.

Before you move to consequences, you must be able to look yourself in the mirror and say:

"I have done everything I can to make this person successful."

If you can't say that honestly, then the issue isn't just their performance. The issue is your leadership.

New Employees and Struggling Employees Need the Same Thing

This applies to both new employees and those who have been struggling for a while.

New hires need structure, clarity, and presence. They must know what's expected, who they can approach for help, and what success looks like in the first 30, 60, and 90 days.

Underperformers need coaching, not just a countdown clock to termination. These employees require specific feedback, realistic goals, and someone who cares enough to walk alongside them for a period of time.

If they've never received the tools, training, and coaching, you don't have the right to say, "They just can't cut it."

You haven't earned that conclusion yet.

The Mirror Test of Leadership

A simple test I use is what I call 'The Mirror Test.' Before I finalize any tough decision about an employee, I ask myself:

- Did I invest in them?
- Did I communicate clearly?
- Did I provide the tools and support they needed?
- Did I make time, or did I hide behind being "too busy"?

If I can answer "yes" to all of these, then I can move forward with a clear conscience. If I can't, then I have work to do because leadership starts with looking in the mirror, not pointing out the window.

Candy: The Employee Who "Wasn't Working Out"

Here's a perfect example of why the mirror test matters.

I once took over a new region and visited a location I hadn't seen before. When I arrived, the manager, let's call him Rick, was sitting outside on a bench waiting for me.

As soon as he saw me, he pulled me aside and said, "I've got someone I'm going to let go."

I replied, "Just so you know, I'll always ask a few questions before we terminate an employee. When we hire someone, we commit to doing everything we can to make them successful. They're feeding their families and taking care of themselves and others. So, we need to be sure before making that kind of decision."

"Okay," he said.

"So, tell me about this person."

He said, "Her name is Candice. She's been with us for about five months. She's not achieving her goals. She's not selling enough diamonds."

I began my questions.

"Has Candy gone through the new employee orientation program?"

"No."

"Has she completed the diamond certification training?"

"No."

"Why not?"

"I just haven't had time to do the training."

She hadn't gone through orientation or diamond certification...and we're surprised her diamond sales are low?

I continued.

"Let's pull out her customer service book," I said. That's where they track daily sales and keep performance objective sheets.

"When I open it to the middle where we record performance objectives, will it be completely filled out? When I flip to the inside, will I see four weekly reviews for the month, one for each week, where you provided feedback on her performance, what she's doing well, where she needs to improve, and what training you scheduled?"

He looked at me and admitted, "No. I haven't had time to do that either."

So here's what we really had:

- No orientation.
- No product certification.
- No documented weekly coaching.

And the plan was to fire her for "not making her numbers."

I told Rick, "You need to look in the mirror. You must ensure you've done everything possible to help her succeed before deciding she can't do the job."

Short story long, and long story short, after receiving the right tools and training, Candy didn't just improve; she became one of the *top-selling sales associates in the* company.

Her performance soared, and she earned additional commissions each month for her achievements. As a single mother striving to provide for her family, she flourished with the support she received.

Candy didn't change who she was; Rick changed how he led.

He learned a vital lesson that I want every leader to grasp: You haven't earned the right to let someone go if you haven't truly given them the tools, training, and coaching to succeed.

Now, contrast that with another situation.

While you seek out good people and work to develop them, you must also recognize when someone on your team simply isn't going to make it. If you inherit individuals with the wrong attitude, it doesn't matter how long they've been there, poor attitudes lead to poor results.

One Christmas season, I inherited a manager with a dreadful attitude. He resisted everything I asked of him and couldn't even meet a simple expectation: submitting his numbers by 5:00 p.m. each day. He acted as if he were busier and more important than the rest of the team.

At that time in the jewelry retail business, 30–35% of annual sales occur between Thanksgiving and the week after Christmas. This all transpired right in the middle of that critical period, the absolute worst time to make a leadership change...at least on paper.

One evening during the holiday rush, I called him to remind him the numbers were due. Not only did he refuse, but he also made a smart comment and used foul language toward our CEO. I informed him that behavior was completely unacceptable. Let's call this employee John.

"If you don't like it, come pick up my keys," John said.

I replied, "John, I'll be there in 13 minutes, and that's if I hit traffic."

Here's the disclaimer: I made that decision on my own. I didn't consult my supervisor or notify corporate in advance. I'm not suggesting that's the proper process; in fact, I encourage you to collaborate with your supervisor and HR when making significant changes like this.

But in that moment of my career, I acted based on what I believed the team and the business needed.

I grabbed the assistant manager, who had been working hard and was ready for more responsibility, gave him a "battlefield promotion," and drove to the location.

John was standing in the middle of the mall, pale as a ghost, keys in his right hand. I approached him, he dropped the keys into my hand, and shook my hand in disbelief that I had actually come.

You can't be afraid to make tough decisions when necessary, even if the timing feels uncomfortable.

If the results hadn't turned out as they did, I would have likely faced serious consequences.

But the results *did* come.

That location performed at a significantly higher level. Team members approached me to express their gratitude, revealing that John had treated them poorly, leaving them unmotivated under his leadership. Everything changed when a leader with the right attitude took over.

The store eventually became the *number-one performing location*, and there were a few laughs, along with a big smile, when my bonus check was handed to me.

That's the other side of *people, people, people*:

- You invest deeply in the right individuals.
- You give every reasonable chance to those who struggle.
- And when the attitude is toxic and consistent, you take action—because the rest of the team is watching.

Putting Your People First Isn't Soft. It's Smart

Putting people first doesn't equate to being lenient on performance. It involves building performance the right way.

When you consistently hire, train, coach, and equip people effectively, something powerful occurs:

- Turnover drops.
- Morale rises.
- Customer experience improves.
- And the KPIs everyone loves to discuss finally start moving in the right direction.

That's why, in my view, the foundation of any successful organization isn't a spreadsheet or a strategy document; it's people.

If you take care of your people, they will take care of your customers, and your numbers will speak for themselves.

At the end of the day, while real estate may be about *location, location, location*, leadership will always center on *people, people, people*.

Once people are on the team, they should have what they need: tools, training, coaching, feedback, and a leader who can reflect and honestly say, "I've done everything I can to help them succeed."

However, there's a crucial step that comes before all of that:

You can't train, coach, or develop people you never hired.

The Leadership Oxymoron: "I Don't Have Time to Recruit"

Picture this: you're walking through a community, region, or division, and you ask a manager:

"Hey Henry, you've been understaffed for a while. When are we going to onboard someone?"

And Henry responds:

"Honestly, I just haven't had the time to look for people."

That response seems reasonable on the surface, but it's actually an oxymoron.

You're understaffed, meaning you're falling behind on your goals, stressed, and likely working excessive hours. The only way out of that situation is to find more people.

Saying you "don't have time" to recruit is like claiming you're too thirsty to stop for water.

If you don't prioritize recruiting, it's only a matter of time before:

- The business struggles, or
- You're the one being coached out for "failing to hit your numbers."

Not because you were a bad operator, but because you never had enough people on the field.

Staffing is not a side project; **staffing is the job.**

You don't "find" time to recruit; you *make* it.

Saying "I haven't had time" is a choice, not a condition.

You will never accidentally stumble into extra free time and think, "You know what, I guess I'll recruit today."

Everything else will always scream louder than recruiting: the angry family in the lobby, the vendor issue, the blown schedule, the report that was due yesterday.

If you wait until everything is calm to recruit, you'll never recruit.

Great leaders do two things: they block time for recruiting. Put it on the calendar like a meeting with your boss, one hour a week, two hours, whatever it is, protect it. That's when you scan résumés, make calls, set up interviews, and follow up with that fantastic server you met last week.

- They treat recruiting as a key controllable, not an extra. You control how many conversations you start.
- You control how many people you invite in.
- You control how visible your "we're always looking for great people" message is.

When you treat recruiting like oxygen instead of an errand, the tone of the business changes.

Always Be Recruiting: The Hat Never Comes Off

Here's the real secret: it's not just about scheduled time.

You should always have your *recruiting hat* on.

That doesn't mean you walk around with a stack of applications like a walking HR department. It means your eyes are open and your radar is on wherever you go:

- You're at a restaurant, and a server takes great care of you.
- You're at a retail store, and an associate remembers your name and goes the extra mile.
- You're on the phone with a customer service rep who owns the problem and follows through.

Those aren't just "nice moments"; they're leads.

Most people in customer-facing roles never hear, "You're really good at what you do," from anyone who can change their life. So, when a leader says:

"Listen, I really like how you took care of me today. I'm in a similar business, and I'm always looking for people like you. I'd love to talk sometime about opportunities on my team,"

...it's flattering, validating, and it opens a door.

You don't have to promise them a job. You're not hiring them on the spot between the appetizer and the entrée; you're simply planting a seed:

"Here's my card. If you'd ever like to explore a place where that kind of service is really valued, I'd love to interview you and see if we might be a fit."

That's it. Thirty seconds. But if you do that consistently, you will never "run out of people."

The Pipeline Beats the Panic

Leaders who are always recruiting live in a different world than those who only recruit in a panic.

Panic recruiting sounds like this: "We lost two people this week. Put an ad up, call HR, and see what's out there. Just get me bdies."

That's how you end up with warm bodies instead of teammates, and you start the turnover cycle all over again.

Pipeline recruiting looks like this: "We have three great candidates already in our orbit. Let's bring them in, talk to them, and see who fits best."

You're always better off when you have a strong bench.

The ideal time to recruit is before desperation strikes. When your team is stable and strong, you can be selective. You can take your time to protect company culture and values, not just ask, "Can this person fog a mirror and pass a background check?"

You earn that luxury only by recruiting while things seem okay on the surface.

A Living Example: "Fresh Hot Pizza"

When I was a regional manager in the jewelry business, one of my stores was in a mall. Every time I visited that property, I walked past a Sbarro in the food court. The manager there, a young man named Michael Maggiotto, consistently called out:

"Hey, how about some fresh hot pizza? Fresh hot pizza today?"

He didn't just shout into the void; he made eye contact and remembered my name from earlier visits.

Most people would have kept walking, thinking, "That guy's pretty good at his job." I saw something deeper; I saw *will*.

You've probably heard the phrase: "Hire for will, train for skill."

I believed that then, and I believe it now. More than 15 years later, it remains a textbook example of why that philosophy works.

After several "fresh hot pizza" pitches and smiles, I stopped, approached Michael, and said:

"I really like how you engage people. I'd love to interview you for our management training program."

He didn't hesitate.

"Absolutely," he replied. "When should we do it?"

We scheduled it for that Saturday. Sure enough, Saturday arrived, and Michael showed up on time, in a sharp suit, ready to go. That alone told me a lot.

During the interview, I explained how our management training program worked, detailing that it could take up to nine months to complete and outlining the expectations. He listened carefully, then said:

"That sounds great. You say it takes up to nine months. I'm going to finish it in six months or less."

That's will. Nobody can teach that.

I hired him into the program.

He didn't just complete it, he excelled. He became one of my highest-performing managers. I started him in a lower-volume store, where he succeeded. I moved him to a medium-volume store, and he succeeded again.

Eventually, I placed him in the highest-volume flagship store in the company, and he delivered there too.

Same person.
Different locations.
Same result: *success.*

That's what happens when you hire for will and then provide the tools, training, and coaching to build the skill.

Now, here's the key point for this chapter:

I never would have had Michael on my team if I'd been "too busy" to notice him.

I could have walked by that Sbarro, convincing myself with the same excuse many managers use: "I don't have time to recruit right now. I've got a hundred other things on my plate."

We all have a hundred things to juggle. That will never change.

Here is what separates great leaders from the rest:

- They keep their recruiting hat on, in the mall, at lunch, or at the coffee shop.
- They act when they see talent, instead of merely thinking, "That person's good."
- They prioritize recruiting and development, rather than waiting to "find" the time that never appears.

If you want successful people, you must be willing to invest time upfront, spotting them, talking to them, interviewing them, and developing them once they join your team.

Using "I don't have the time" as an excuse is unacceptable.

If you never make the time, you'll never have the people. And if you never have the people, you'll never achieve the results.

About the Author

Alex Hernandez is a dynamic and results-driven executive leader with an entrepreneurial spirit.

He grew up in Fayetteville, North Carolina, as the son of an immigrant and a three-war veteran. Hard work and the importance of human connection were lessons Alex learned at a young age. As soon as he was old enough, Alex enlisted in the United States Air Force. He became one of the youngest airmen to represent McChord Air Force Base in a worldwide base competition and went on to serve during Operation Desert Storm.

Alex earned a Bachelor of Science in Business Management from the University of North Carolina at Pembroke, where he was active in student leadership and multiple organizational initiatives. He also holds an Associate of Applied Science in Transportation Management from the Community College of the Air Force, completed during his active and reserve military service—an experience that reinforced his values of discipline, teamwork and service.

Alex believes a strong culture empowers a team to create lasting success. His background in entrepreneurship shaped his leadership philosophy—bold, strategic and deeply relationship-centered.

Throughout Alex's professional career, he has led multimillion-dollar enterprises through complex transformations, revitalized underperforming operations and guided teams to exceed ambitious growth objectives. His leadership has repeatedly produced double-digit increases in revenue, sales and team engagement while cultivating organizational cultures that inspire innovation and accountability. At the core of his leadership is a passion for the transformation of people, performance and businesses.

CHAPTER TWELVE

Use Disney's Influence Strategies for the Happiest Bottom-Line on Earth

By Robert J. Smith, MFA

The influence strategies that enable the massive Disney corporation to turn experiences into billions annually can also help you grow, whether you lead a team of five or five hundred. In this chapter, you'll receive a practical overview of seven proven influence strategies, a Disney example for each, and straightforward ways to apply them to your marketing and sales starting today. You don't need a Disney-sized budget; you need Disney-level intention.

I previously discussed Walt's prolific storytelling in INFLUENCE IN ACTIONTM GAINS PROVEN RESULTS AND DRIVES SALES.

Now, whether you embark on this journey alone or with support later, the principle remains the same: influence is a skill set that can be learned. Let's break down the strategies Disney employs and how you can implement them immediately in your own business.

Whichever route you take, ensure that your company's stories are compelling and persuade people to engage with you. There is no substitute for **Factual StorytellingTM**. None.

Factual Storytelling™ consists of proof, results, and measured outcomes, along with before-and-after realities. These verifiable elements create a compelling narrative that makes the truth easy to grasp and hard to overlook. Factual Storytelling™ simplifies complex issues through engaging dialogue. Humans are inherently drawn to stories and inspired by them, a tendency that has persisted throughout our shared history. With Factual Storytelling™, you can transition from vague assertions of 'we're the best' to concrete examples of how other customers and clients transformed their problems into proven strategies, leading to measurable improvements.

Here is your quickest route to success with Factual Storytelling™:

Utilize tried-and-true strategies of influence, just as Disney did and continues to do. Some of the most effective strategies include:

Affiliation and Unity – I've witnessed the power of affiliation firsthand. Disney's sponsorships, past and present, foster a sense of shared identity that benefits Disney, the sponsors, and the guests. When customers feel part of something larger, they don't just make a single purchase; they develop a sense of belonging, which fosters loyalty.

Authority and Credibility – Walt Disney received 26 Academy Awards for his contributions to film. Among these were 22 competitive Oscars out of 59 nominations, along with 4 honorary Oscars. No one else has come close to matching this level of recognition. Few company founders are held in such high regard by their peers.

Disney continues to employ the brilliant storytelling techniques of its founder, Walt Disney. During his lifetime, he won 21 competitive Academy Awards for his storytelling prowess and vision, plus a posthumous Oscar for **_Winnie the Pooh and the Blustery Day_**, _bringing_ his total to 22.

Walt also received several honorary Academy Awards during his life. One was an honorary statuette for creating Mickey Mouse, the world's most recognizable mascot (awarded in 1932). Another was for **Snow White and the Seven Dwarfs**, **"recognized as a significant screen innovation which has charmed millions and pioneered a great new entertainment field for the motion picture cartoon"** (1939).

He also received an award alongside William Garity, John N. A. Hawkins, and the Radio Corporation of America (RCA), "for their outstanding contribution to the advancement of the use of sound in motion pictures through the production of Fantasia." Finally, Walt was honored with the Irving G. Thalberg Memorial Award, given to "creative producers whose bodies of work reflect a consistently high quality of motion picture production."

As of 2025, the company is ranked **#46** on the Fortune 500 list. [source: https://www.50pros.com/fortune500]

Commitment and Consistency – Disney leverages its extensive catalogue of intellectual property to create new experiences tied to proven franchises. This approach strengthens the brand and makes new attractions and merchandise appealing to a broad audience. More on intellectual property is discussed later in this chapter.

Walt's legendary commitment to storytelling is evident in his company's relentless production of animated films, documentaries, books, comics, music, and television shows, interrupted only by their direct assistance to the U.S. government during World War II.

Liking and Being Liked – To boost sales, revenues, and profits, becoming likeable is essential. One way to achieve this is by genuinely appreciating your customers and consistently delivering quality solutions, products, and services. Another approach is to master the art of storytelling. If you're not a master storyteller, consider becoming one, hiring one, or engaging a consulting firm that excels in storytelling.

Disney enhances park and resort experiences through character dining and a more subtle method: removing dollar signs from menus. Additionally, using guest "magic bands" for payment transforms the spending experience. It's remarkable how much money people spend when they simply wave their wrist across a card reader, eliminating cash and card transactions.

Reciprocity and Rapport – Complimentary "1st Visit," "I'm Celebrating," "Happily Ever After," and "Happy Birthday!" pins, personalized by cast members, foster reciprocity and create rapport among guests and between guests and cast members.

Many cast members and guests go out of their way to make pin-wearers feel welcome and appreciated. This thoughtful gesture spreads joy and goodwill, making it easier for people to spend money when they are in a good mood.

Scarcity and Limited Opportunity – In essence, scarcity means undersupply. It's crucial to remember that authenticity is key for scarcity to be effective. Even when we recognize this strategy's influence, we often make purchases before it's too late. However, false scarcity is unethical and is frequently misused in sales tactics, such as perpetual "Going Out of Business" sales, unnecessary "Act Now" prompts, and "Sale ends at Midnight" claims when items remain available afterward.

Here is a legitimate Disney tactic that worked on me on my birthday at EPCOT, just four days before this writing: After Sharon treated me to a fine dinner at Le Cellier in the Canada pavilion, we stopped for some delicious maple corn to take home for football-watching the rest of the weekend. The popcorn vendor had a Stitch popcorn bucket at the register that we had never seen before. Stitch was dressed as a mummy, trick-or-treating with a (plastic) candy in one hand and an overflowing pumpkin filled with (plastic) candy in the other.

What caught my attention was a handwritten note on a small slip of paper that read **"LAST BUCKET OF THE DAY!"** I asked the young lady, "Last bucket of the day, or last bucket period?" Her response was perfect. "It's the last one we have, and with Halloween less than a week away, we won't be restocking. You may find one at another stand, but we won't have any more here." I had two reasons for responding **"SOLD!"** Stitch is our daughter's favorite character, and Sharon and I had already walked ten miles through the park. With the last one right in front of me, there was no chance we were not buying it then and there.

Social Proof and Certainty – Nothing sells like certainty. Disney bridges the gap from uncertainty to certainty through social proof, encouraging user-generated content for word-of-mouth advertising at no cost, along with high-profile endorsements from Super Bowl MVPs.

Here is an example of both from earlier tonight:

As mentioned, Sharon and I went to EPCOT to see Big Bad Voodoo Daddy perform three sets at the American Gardens Theatre. We sat front and center in the main section next to someone who was live streaming the show. Disney doesn't discourage what was once termed 'bootlegging'; in fact, the company embraces it. You can barely walk through any Disney Park without encountering scores of influencers and wannabe influencers.

As for mega influencers, such as Super Bowl MVPs, Michigan quarterback Tom Brady has won the award five times, four with the New England Patriots and once with our Tampa Bay Buccaneers.

You know the bit from the television ads. Disney's signature jingle plays, **"When you wish upon a star..."** and we hear an off-screen announcer: Tom Brady and Rob Gronkowski, you and the Tampa Bay Buccaneers have just won the Super Bowl. What are you going to do?

Brady and Gronk: We're going to Disney World!

Why does Disney invest heavily in endorsements from Super Bowl MVPs? Most football fans think, "If it's good enough for Tom Brady, it's good enough for me." This mindset shifts millions of football enthusiasts and casual Super Bowl viewers from uncertainty to certainty. Yes, EPCOT was packed tonight, just as I expect all other Disney parks were.

Disney reportedly spends billions on marketing each year. As demonstrated in the previous scarcity example, even a small sale can be made with just a pen, a piece of scrap paper, and a bit of ingenuity.

One effective way to instill certainty in your prospects is through celebrity endorsements. You don't need to pay Super Bowl MVP rates like Disney does. For instance, when Kevin Harrington, an original shark on ***ABC's Shark Tank,*** endorsed me, it was natural and cost me nothing. Consider who in your network might be willing to endorse you. If no one comes to mind, reach out to us. We can help you secure the endorsements you need. While we may be able to connect you with anyone you want, such endorsements might come at a higher price than you anticipate. If that's the case, we'll find the right endorsement that fits your budget.

An ethical note: endorsements must be genuine. If money or perks are exchanged, disclose those facts. Never imply outcomes that aren't typical for your customers and clients, and don't borrow credibility you haven't earned. My guiding principle has always been, "Earn everything." Influence is powerful, use it ethically and frequently.

As I've always asked my children when they wanted something beyond their financial reach, "What does Mick Jagger say?" Their answer is always the same: **"You can't always get what you want. But if you try sometime, well, you just might find, you get what you need."**

The sky is the limit for what you can achieve by applying the proven principles discussed in this chapter. Whether you increase sales by $30 at no expense, as in the case of the popcorn bucket, or by $30,000,000 or more, as Disney does regularly, the choice is yours.

Untapped influence adds nothing to your bottom line. In contrast, **INFLUENCE IN ACTIONTM** can transform a noncompetitive business into a competitive one, and **it** can elevate a competitive business to industry dominance.

"I have been up against tough competition all my life. I wouldn't know how to get along without it."
— **Walt Disney**

Here's a bonus strategy that Disney employs: devices known as **"Smellitizers."** You can't walk down Main Street without the enticing aroma of popcorn and baked goods wafting through the air, conveniently available in stores, gift shops, kiosks, and quick-service restaurants. These enticing scents come from pressurized air tanks that pump through vents. **"Smellitizers"** are even activated at precise moments, such as the apple pie scent released over the audience during the Be Our Guest scene of the PhilharMagic attraction.

https://www.businessinsider.com/disney-smellitzer-how-disneyland-uses-smells-to-influence-visitors-2023-9. 9-19-23

- Make the experience easy on the senses: Use clean designs, clear signage, and smooth customer paths. Less friction equals more business.

- Employ on-brand environmental cues (music, lighting, packaging, sampling, where appropriate) to reinforce the feelings you want your customers to remember.

- Keep it honest: you're not manipulating people, you're enhancing the environment so that the experiences you provide match the promises you make.

A similar tactic is used by real estate agents and home sellers during FSBO home showings and open houses, with fresh cookies baking in the oven. You can adopt this same technique as a Fortune 100 company for the small cost of freshly baked cookies.

And of course, there's the tried-and-true **"Exit through the gift shop"** strategy. When is a better time to purchase gifts that embody the memory of an attraction than in the moment of experiencing that thrill?

The same principle applies to your clients. With every sale, you should consistently offer an upgrade or companion/add-on sale. At the very least, your satisfied clients will know what's available to them and to the friends and family they refer to you. Never pressure a customer or client, and never do them the disservice of failing to inform them about their options.

Dare to be Different

This is where influence transitions from mere theory to the execution of business strategy. Differentiation is how you apply influence, by making complex issues clear, easy to understand, and memorable, you can shift people from 'maybe' to 'yes.' Confused minds always say no. Our role is to bring clarity and certainty, allowing people to trust their decisions and achieve the results they desire.

In 1934, few believed that adults would sit through a full-length animated film. Disney thought differently when he retold the Brothers Grimm fairy tale, *Snow White and the Seven Dwarfs.* In an interview, he recounted, **"It was prophesized that nobody would sit through a cartoon an hour and a half long. But we had decided there was only one way we could successfully do** *Snow White:* **it was 'go for broke,' 'shoot the works.' There could be no compromise on money, talent, or time."**

While his original budget was $250,000, it ultimately exceeded $1 million, a substantial amount for 1934. The film grossed $8.5 million upon its initial release, making it the highest-grossing film of its time. *Snow White* was re-released in theaters multiple times, increasing the total box-office gross to approximately $185 million. Even after adjusting for inflation and factoring in video, DVD, and merchandising sales, Walt's bold decision to take a risk on something unprecedented paid off. Given that studios typically recoup 40% to 50% of box office revenue, that $1 million investment conservatively transformed into $74 million.

Differentiation is Your Key to Success

To ensure our business's survival and eventual industry dominance, we must embrace uniqueness in our marketing, advertising, sales methods, and content. **"In advertising, not to be different is virtually suicidal." - William Bernbach, founder of the international advertising agency, Doyle Dane Bernbach (DDB)**

Consider this example: I was involved in a complex estate planning case where major players in the financial services industry spent six months pressuring an elderly couple, convincing them that their firm had the best solution to an impending tax issue that threatened to cripple their estate and devastate their heirs.

Half a dozen Fortune 500 companies sent teams of investment advisors, life insurance agents, attorneys, and accountants with lengthy and complicated financial plans that only confused the couple. One financial services giant after another failed to close the deal, leaving the couple with an unresolved, significant problem.

Recognizing that a confused mind always says "No," I aimed to simplify their complex issue. Thus, *INSURANCEMAN* was born. With just a blank legal pad and a pencil, I crafted an engaging Superman-style story illustrating how *INSURANCEMAN* could help them solve their problem for pennies on the dollar.

Before I finished the story, the husband slammed his fist on my desk, startling his wife. He exclaimed, "Now, I finally understand it!" His wife began to cry and nodded in agreement, saying, "I understand it as well." That twenty minutes together was invaluable for all three of us. Their massive problem was finally resolved, and my reward was an additional $110,000 commission on top of my previous fees earned from addressing their other financial challenges.

No matter your industry, I can create a persuasive marketing and sales comic for you by writing it and having it illustrated by our MARVEL Comics, DC Comics, and newspaper comic strip artists. Regardless of your customer needs, we can deliver this for under $10,000. If you replicate my approach, your investment could yield an eleven-fold return. How many 11X investments have you made in your business over the past year? If you can achieve an 11X return on a small investment once, how many times can you repeat that success? Consider how easy it is to invest less than $10,000 today compared to the $1 million Disney invested in 1934, which is equivalent to over $24 million today.

Comic books are an effective way to convey complex ideas and solutions to prospective customers. Before handing over a lengthy report that prospects may never read, consider providing an 8-page sales comic that they can digest in just a few minutes. While *INSURANCEMAN* took me twenty minutes to explain from scratch, your prospects can easily read a similar story in three to four minutes and *instantly grasp the key points you want to* communicate.

Here's the best part: there's no better referral piece than a **Factual Storytelling™** marketing and sales comic in the hands of your satisfied clients. It's remarkable how many clients will share these with friends and family when you provide them with a sufficient supply. The long shelf-life of sales comics is another reason no business should be without them. When you give out expensive brochures, how long do they stay in your prospects' hands? A day or two at best, if they don't end up in the circular file the moment you leave their sight. In contrast, when I conduct annual reviews with clients, they always have their original copy of *THE ADVENTURES OF INSURANCEMAN* with them, year after year.

"Fantasy, that is good, acceptable fantasy,
is really only fact, with a whimsical twist."
— **Walt Disney**

Always retain the intellectual assets you create and secure lifetime licensing for any content developed for you. After inadvertently signing away the rights to his creation, Oswald the Lucky Rabbit, and losing the character in a poor production deal, Disney vowed never to make the same mistake again. With the mindset of a future CEO, Disney declared, **"Never again will I work for anyone else."**

Shortly after losing Oswald in 1927, Walt Disney created one of the most successful mascots in history: Mickey Mouse, in 1928. Recognizing the value of intellectual assets, the Walt Disney Company executed a remarkable trade. In 2006, nearly 80 years after Walt lost the rights to Oswald, Disney traded sportscaster Al Michaels to Universal Studios to regain those rights for Oswald, the Lucky Rabbit.

As for me, I own all the rights to ***INSURANCEMAN, SHORT ATTENTION SPAN DAN*** and a collection of other intellectual properties. Take inventory of your intellectual assets and protect them; you'll be glad you did.

You may have more intellectual assets than you realize. Consider everything from your logo to your company mascot.

You do have a corporate mascot, don't you? When you think about how Mickey Mouse generated $171 billion for the Walt Disney Company over 95 years before the character's copyright recently expired, it becomes clear that you're missing out without one. To add insult to injury, that boat is being piloted by Steamboat Willie himself.

Disney has reported that 98% of children aged 3–11 worldwide recognize Mickey Mouse. More children likely know Mickey than Santa Claus. Imagine the impact this recognition has on the company's brand. Now picture what an effective mascot could do for your brand. If you don't have a company mascot, now is the time to create one. Our Marvel and DC Comics freelancers can help you develop one. [source: https://www.50pros.com/fortune500 9-1-2025]

If you lack a mascot, make its creation *priority one*. Put our MARVEL Comics and DC Comics artists to work for you *immediately*. Your mascot might not generate $171 billion or even $171 million, but if it brings in an extra $171,000 for the minimal cost of production, it would be foolish not to create it.

The same goes for your jingle. Disney's "When You Wish Upon a Star" jingle has become a staple of the company's commercials.

Here is something I wrote on the value of jingles as a member of the Forbes Business Council: https://www.forbes.com/councils/forbes businesscouncil/2023/12/13/jingle-all-the-way-to-the-bank-why-your-business-needs-a-strong-jingle/

Here is our jingle: https://patriotsmith.pro/4qD5CAR

Our jingle has performed wonders for us, generating revenues that far exceed the modest production cost. A jingle can do the same for you and your company.

"Mickey Mouse to me, is the symbol of independence. Born of necessity, the little fellow literally freed us of immediate worry. He provided the means for expanding our organization to its present dimensions and for extending the medium of cartoon animation toward new entertainment levels."

— **Walt Disney**

You don't have to be in entertainment, like the Walt Disney Company, to benefit from a corporate mascot that helps sell your products and services. Whether you sell tires like the Michelin Man, fast food like Ronald

McDonald, cereal like Tony the Tiger, tuna like Charlie, vegetables like The Jolly Green Giant, or cleaning supplies like Mr. Clean, a corporate mascot can enhance your brand.

Here's how we developed ours: https://www.forbes.com/councils/forbesbusinesscouncil/2023/08/23/requiem-for-a-heavyweight-tagline-how-to-create-one-for-your-business/

We can develop yours as well. When we do, you gain another valuable asset that boosts your bottom line. The best part about intellectual assets is their versatility; you can repurpose them across various mediums to generate income.

For example, your mascot can feature in print ads, radio spots, television commercials, and online promotions. It can appear in books, magazines, and comic books, as well as on your corporate campus and special events. The possibilities for your mascot to contribute to your success are limitless.

Getting things done, on time, means everything to your customers and clients. When you consistently deliver, your clients know they can rely on you, leading to repeat business. When they trust that you will deliver for them, they also trust you with referrals. We build trust through actions, not just words. The most effective way to establish trust is to set deadlines for the results you promise.

"Everybody needs deadlines. Even the beavers. They loaf around all summer, but when they are faced with the winter deadline, they work like fury. If we didn't have deadlines, we'd stagnate."
— Walt Disney

By keeping your word and consistently delivering, you won't lose business based on price. People are willing to pay a premium for dependability, as the peace of mind it brings is always worth the cost.

If you want help implementing these strategies quickly, story creation, messaging, endorsements, IP development, or building a comprehensive influence-based marketing system, our team is here to support you. If that sounds like you, reach out, and we'll map the fastest path from your current message to a clear, scalable influence engine.

Your One-Day Influence Plan (Do This Today):

1. Write one proof-based story from your business (problem → solution → result).

2. Gather three pieces of social proof (testimonials, reviews, case metrics).

3. Create one ethical scarcity offer (limited seats, dates, or quantity) *that actually exists*. This should never be manufactured; if it isn't truthful, it isn't ethical.

4. Add one reciprocity touch (a small service, a bonus, or an early onboarding perk).

5. Strengthen authority (a #1 Best Selling book, a television interview, a magazine feature, a podcast appearance, or citing case stats).

6. Improve likability by simplifying pricing and menu language, thereby removing friction. For example, Disney has successfully eliminated dollar signs ($) from their dining menus.

7. Draft a pitch for an affiliation partnership that highlights a shared audience and mutual benefits.

8. Repeat your strongest message for consistency across three channels to make a significant impact.

Essentials:

- Build affiliations through partnerships that foster shared successes.
- Strengthen **authority** with real proof, credentials, and measurable outcomes.

- Maintain **consistency** by repeating effective IP/messages across multiple channels.
- Enhance likability by genuinely serving customers and simplifying their buying experience.
- Trigger **reciprocity** with small, thoughtful gestures that people appreciate and want to share with others. This approach is essential for delivering value and inspiring customers to encourage their friends and family to experience similar benefits from your company.
- Use **scarcity** only when it's genuine, avoiding gimmicks to distinguish yourself from competitors.
- Leverage **social proof** to help individuals transition from uncertainty to confidence, certainty drives sales.
- Differentiate by making complex concepts understandable, creating an impact that prompts prospects to take immediate action.
- Protect your intellectual assets, own what you create.

Resources: We are here to help you implement proven strategies to increase your sales, revenues, and profits.

Book your complimentary consultation here to discover what we can do for you:

https://SmithProfits.com/Contact

About The Author

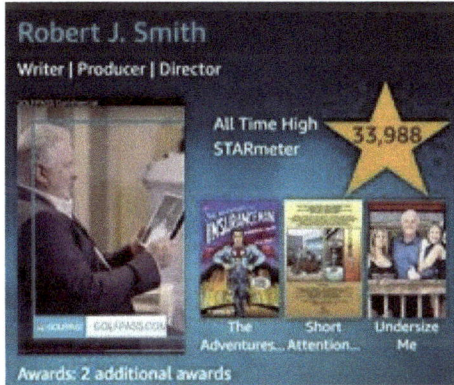

Robert J. Smith, MFA has authored and co-authored several #1 Best Selling books. He's earned numerous #1 rankings sales production and set numerous records with multiple Fortune 500 Companies. Smith has consistently ranked in the top 1% in financial services worldwide, and in the Internet Movie Database (IMDb), out of roughly 15,000,000 people listed. Robert J. Smith Productions is also an "IMDb Top 5,000 Company."

Smith and his companies also consistently rank at the very top of the front page of Google Searches, besting a former NFL running back by the same name, and even a Rock and Roll Hall of Fame front man, with the same name and the same middle initial. He also ranks in the top 1% in his industry and in the top 1% in his vast network on LinkedIn, according to that site's Social Selling Index (SSI). **Most importantly, Smith's consulting work helps his clients accomplish some, or all of the above, as they need it.**

SCAN ME

> *"Anything that won't sell, I don't want to invent.*
> *Its sale is proof of utility, and utility is success."*
> — **Thomas A. Edison**

Epilogue

"To do more for the world than the world does for you – that is success."
— **Henry Ford**

You now have a clear playbook to boost your sales, revenues, and profits. You've learned how to think, plan, and execute with purpose. When you apply these lessons consistently, your results will exceed expectations. If you ever need an extra set of eyes or a quick assist, feel free to reach out to any of our accomplished co-authors directly. If you encounter any difficulties contacting them, let me know, and I will facilitate that for you.

Once your business is thriving, it's time to give back, starting in your own community. I've volunteered for decades in every state I've lived in, and now I'm focused on inspiring achievement in America's youth while bringing families together. We're launching our efforts with students to celebrate our nation's 250th birthday, starting in Florida, with plans to serve children and families in all 50 states and every U.S. territory.

Whether you want to start your own charity, as I did, or continue supporting causes you care about, that choice is yours. Do what you can, with what you have, where you are. No one can reasonably ask for more from you, me, or anyone else.

And remember: giving back isn't just about donating money. One of the most valuable contributions you can make is your time, attention, and guidance, especially to young people who need direction and encouragement. By offering these resources, you will witness remarkable progress in the lives of those you serve.

Here are several examples of how to support young Americans who seek direction and encouragement, particularly in these turbulent times when leadership, confidence, clarity, and achievement are in short supply:

1. I've volunteered to teach entrepreneurship pitching skills to students in middle schools, high schools, and universities. We've consistently produced state champions who have earned sponsorships and awards ranging from $2,000 to $10,000. More importantly, I've seen students realize that their ideas, voices, and newfound skills can open real doors for them.

2. I also volunteer to teach public speaking to elementary school students. It's been rewarding to witness young learners improve their lives through the confidence they gain by stepping outside their comfort zones. We teach them how to prepare, work efficiently, conquer their nerves, and communicate with clarity, skills that benefit them in all areas of life.

3. Another way to assist young people is through our **Junior Patriots™** nonprofit. While tax-deductible donations are welcome, our primary mission is to promote service-minded citizenship and create real opportunities for youth.

Nothing is handed to them. Students earn their success, starting with a simple essay.

We are always looking for public and private schools, homeschool networks, and youth organizations to partner with, including youth sports leagues, scouts, and others. For students who are homeschooled or unaffiliated with a participating organization, we create anthologies to ensure every young person in America has the opportunity to participate, learn, and grow.

If you want to help, you can support local schools and youth groups by inviting us to speak to students and families. We also offer opportunities for you to sponsor students. Feel free to contact us and connect us with any school or youth organization in your area that could benefit from our program.

You can even set your own children up for success while teaching them about patriotism and achievement. Join them in this educational project to strengthen your family's bond.

For those students who are homeschooled or unaffiliated with a participating youth organization, we create anthologies to ensure every young person can engage. By participating, you can teach your children about patriotism while bringing your family closer together.

Success isn't just what you build; it's also what you create and pass on. Success is your legacy. You now have the tools to grow your business, establish stability for your family, and lead with intention. Use what you've learned to uplift others because that kind of success endures. That kind of success is generational. Wishing you and yours all the best.

https://JuniorPatriots.us

"We want something educational, something to keep the family together that would be a credit to the community, to the country as a whole."
— **Walt Disney**

Become a #1 Best Selling Author in our #1 Best Selling INFLUENCE IN ACTIONTM series.

Whether you are a CEO, or a professional with something to offer, feel free to contact me for your own chapter in one of our upcoming books, so that you may become a **#1 Best Selling Author.** You'll immediately be able to increase your credibility and authority to increase your income.

If you are a public speaker, you will find yourself to be even more in demand than you already are. You'll not only increase your fees per presentation you'll increase the amount of speaking gigs that you are able to book. Not only that, you'll find that your audience engagement begins to boom, and your sales closing ratios will skyrocket to optimal rates.

Here is an example: I recently attended a three-day conference that many of my clients attend, here in Orlando. One speaker after another got up onstage and I noticed the same thing, day after day, after day.

When people 2,000 – 3,000 attendees sat down at various ten-top tables, they immediately began talking, drinking coffee and eating pastries. Some immediately got onto their computers, or other electronic devices, oblivious to what was going on around them.

When speakers were introduced, nothing changed. People kept eating, drinking, working, and even worse, they continued talking. All this when they should have been paying attention to the professional onstage.

By comparison, when speakers were introduced as **#1 Best Selling Authors**, everything changed. The food and drinks were immediately set down. Electronic devices were closed, except for attendees taking notes, and everyone sat up straight, to pay attention. Some sat up straight and tall, with pen and notepad in hand.

Each speaker who was introduced as a **#1 Best Selling Author** had 2,000 – 3,000 potential clients engaged and ready to buy. Each of them was surrounded by prospects the minute they walked offstage, as well.

The difference between speakers introduced as **#1 Best Selling Authors** and those who were not, was like night and day. The audience reaction was not only consistent, day after day, I saw the exact same thing happen at several conferences, since.

See if you notice the same thing, the next time you are at a local or national conference. I'll be amazed if you don't.

If you want the same authority and respect that being a **#1 Best Selling Author** provides to you, whether you speak to audiences or not, contact me. You can either write a chapter in our **#1 Best Selling Series** or you can write your own book. Either way, we will market you to a **#1 Best Seller.**

SCAN ME

When a prospective customer or client asks you what make you an expert on your industry, you can legitimately say, that you "Wrote the book on it."

About Your INFLUENCE IN ACTION™ Series Creator

ROBERT J. SMITH, MFA

Born in metro Detroit, Smith learned to compete at a young age, winning baseball championships in his first season at the age of nine and in his final season at the age of thirty, including a streak of six out of his first eight seasons, all on eight different teams.

His work ethic was developed in his blue-collar beginnings. No one in the history of Automobile Capital of the World, or in the Great State of Michigan, has completed more oil changes in one day, one week, or one month than Smith has. In fact, he averaged two cars at once from 6:30 a.m. to midnight, seven days per week, for thirty-one straight days during a Mobil Oil recall in the early 1980s.

After moving to Florida, Smith and another route driver teamed up to complete all of their deliveries after every other route truck driver for Coca-Cola was called back into the warehouse during Hurricane Elena. After developing the #1 home market merchandising route in the Sarasota territory, Smith suffered an on-the-job injury which led to a career change into the financial services industry.

As a financial services advisor, Smith reached #1 worldwide rankings at AXA Financial, The Equitable, Mutual of New York (MONY), and BankAtlantic/BB&T/SunTrust/Truist. He set records at John Hancock and New York Life. His name is enshrined in a plaque on Madison Avenue.

https://SmithProfits.com/

Debilitating spine and other severe injuries necessitated a career change. While undergoing multiple surgeries to regain the ability to walk, he concurrently earned his Master of Fine Arts (MFA) in Creative Writing as Valedictorian at Full Sail University, and his Feature Film Writing degree "With Distinction" at UCLA. He holds Director's Awards for "The Art of Visual Storytelling" as well as for "Editing for Film, Games, and Animation."

https://RobertJSmith.com

Smith's consulting practice helps financial advisors reach the top 1% in worldwide production, entertainers reach the top 1% in the Internet Movie Database (IMDb), and every client gain top Google search rankings.

https://RobertJSmithProductions.com

He is an International Best-Selling Author with *SALES GENIUS #1©*, which bested The Wolf of Wall Street's book on sales. *THE ADVENTURES OF INSURANCEMAN©*

increases sales for clients and their companies. Smith created **SHORT ATTENTION SPAN DAN©** to teach writing and public speaking to students.

Robert J. Smith, MFA's Amazon Author Page

After earning his Leadership Certification in Influencing People at the University of Michigan, Smith has turned many businesspeople into #1 International Bestselling Authors.

Smith and his companies have been featured on ABC, CBS, CW, FOX, The Golf Channel, NBC, WGN, and hundreds of other media outlets.

https://www.IMDb.Me/RobertJSmith

He's been named to the Entrepreneur Magazine Leadership Network, the Inc. Leadership Forum, the Fast Company Executive Board, and the Forbes Business Council.

https://www.forbes.com/councils/forbesbusinesscouncil/people /smittyrobertjsmith/

Smith's other book titles in the works include, **#1: HOW TO REACH THE VERY TOP IN YOUR INDUSTRY - NO MATTER YOUR PROFESSION and EVERYTHING YOU ALWAYS WANTED TO ABOUT INCREASING BUSINESS**AND WERE AFRAID TO ASK©.**

https://SmithProfits.com/Books/

Smith raised millions for charity and volunteers in public and private schools. Within 24-hours in 2024, one of his high school students, and one of his medical school students each won their Entrepreneur Pitch

Championships and earned sizable cash prizes to develop each of their medical products that will greatly benefit mankind.

He's served as a Field Councilman for the Greater Detroit Area Life Underwriters, Board Member of the Tampa Bay United Way, Treasurer of World League Baseball, and President of the Executive Sports Council. Smith currently serves as President of the Junior Patriots™ Corp.

He lives in Winter Garden, Florida, with Sharon Roznowski and has three grown children: Ashley, Austin, and Sabrina.

Coming Soon

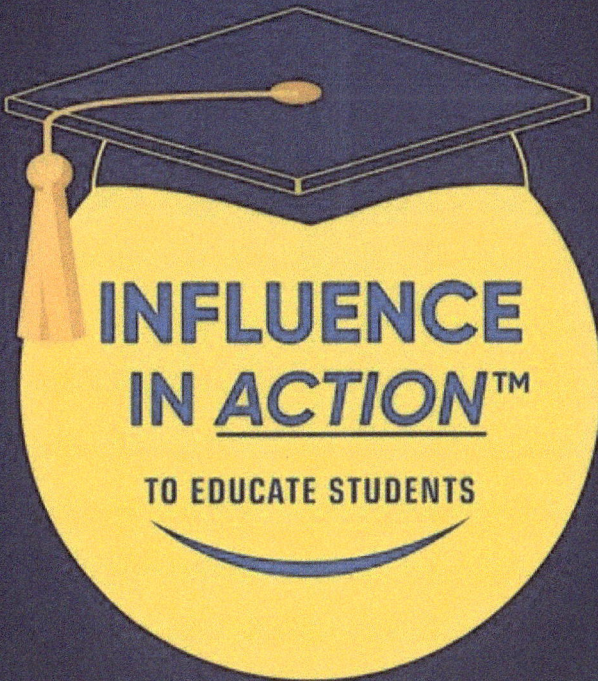

Four Decades of Success with the Big Three and Others

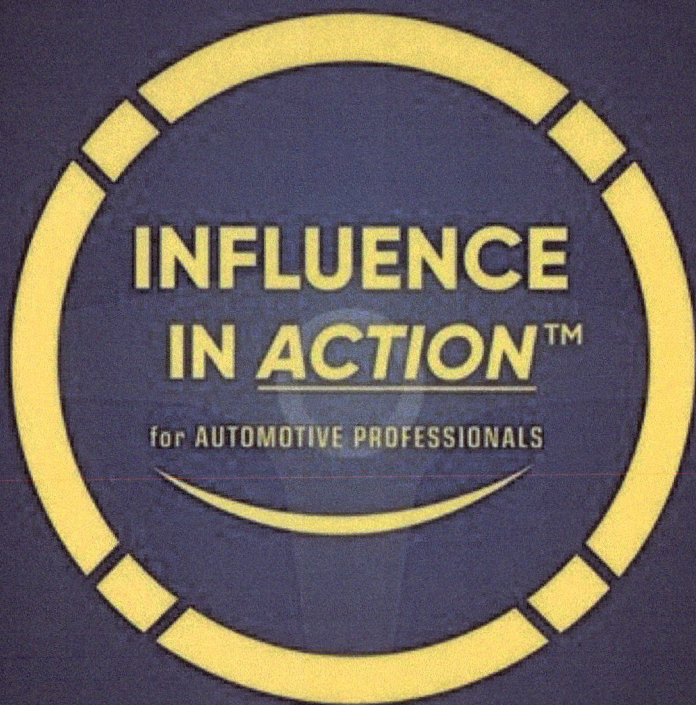

INFLUENCE IN *ACTION*™

for AUTOMOTIVE PROFESSIONALS

**ROBERT J. SMITH, MFA and
Automotive Experts**

Everything you always wanted to know about increasing business*

*AND WERE AFRAID TO ASK

Explained by
Robert J. Smith, MFA
and his Forbes articles

#1
HOW TO REACH THE TOP IN YOUR INDUSTRY
NO MATTER YOUR PROFESSION©
(Cover Coming Soon)

And, our most ambitious project to-date:

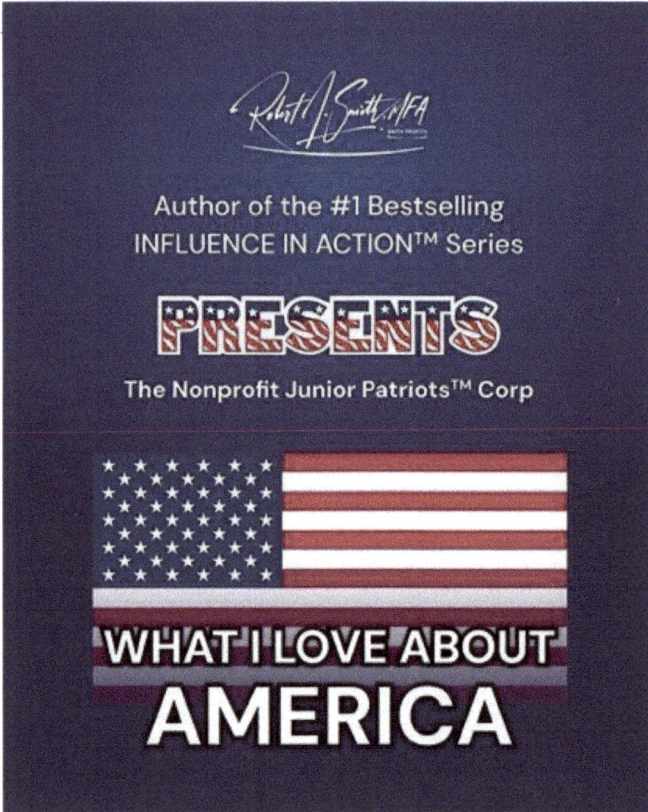

Author of the #1 Bestselling
INFLUENCE IN ACTION™ Series

PRESENTS

The Nonprofit Junior Patriots™ Corp

WHAT I LOVE ABOUT
AMERICA

By the
STUDENTS and FACULTY of
YOUR YOUTH ORGANIZATION HERE

A revolutionary new book series where we will help thousands of students and teachers, plus administrative and support staff to become #1 Best Selling Authors!

Our goal is to encourage American patriotism in 250 public and private schools and youth organizations to celebrate our nations' 250th anniversary.

To become involved and support this project, please feel free to reach out to me direct at (407) 508-0200 and/or Robert@RobertJSmith.com

Thank you.

SCAN ME

https://JuniorPatriots.us

Coming Soon from SMITH COMICS

Upcoming JUNIOR PATRIOTS™ Titles

Upcoming SMITH PROFITS™ Titles
for You to Use in Sales and Marketing,
to Increase Sales, Revenues and Profits:

The Adventures of Insurancewoman©

Real Estate Woman©

Real Estate Man©

The Amazing Website-Man©

The Loan Arranger©

Super Dentist©

Sherry Mason©

The Adventures of Bernie Burns©

And any custom sales and marketing piece to suit your business.

Upcoming SMITH COMICS™ Titles
To Educate Students

SHORT ATTENTION SPAN DAN:
THE GREAT HOUDAN©

SHORT ATTENTION SPAN DAN:
WILD THING, YOU MOVE ME©

Current titles may be found here:
https://www.Amazon.com/Author/RobertJSmith

Book your no cost, initial consultation now at:
https://SmithProfits.com/Contact

Learn how you can eliminate your business problems and optimize all of
your opportunities:
https://SmithProfits.com

SMITHPROFITS.com

WE'LL HAMMER OUT PROFITS FOR YOUR BUSINESS

Robert J. Smith, MFA

SMITH PROFITS

www.ingramcontent.com/pod-product-compliance
Lightning Source LLC
Chambersburg PA
CBHW040917210326
41597CB00030B/5109